The Odin Brotherhood

The Odin Brotherhood

Published by
Mandrake of Oxford
PO Box 250
OXFORD
OX1 1AP (UK)

In Honor of Paul Joseph Mirabello,
the "Master of those who Know"

When the world is pregnant with lies, a secret long hidden will be revealed.

AN ODINIST PROPHECY

Contents

Introduction

This work—written during what Hermann Hesse has called "the end of modern times, shortly before the return of the Middle Ages"—is designed for the student of occult religions. Paganism is a growing force, and I believe a disinterested observer should record and publish some of the material available on the Odin Brotherhood, a mysterious fraternity that is one of the most interesting manifestations of Odinist polytheism.

Because my aim is preservation rather than criticism, I have simply detailed the Brotherhood's beliefs and have made no attempt to scrutinize their "mysteries." At times the ideas relayed to me were unusual in the extreme—doctrines that deify men and humanize gods, legends of magic gates that lead to divine enclaves, prophecies of wars with apocalyptic monsters, clues concerning a treasure trove of golden monoliths, and much more—but I have decided to record these ideas without comment. It is my hope, however, that others will some day evaluate the interesting and perplexing phenomenon that is called Odinism.

Since the Odin Brotherhood is a "secret society," my sources (encountered while I was conducting doctoral research in history at Scotland's University of Glasgow) must remain anonymous, and I therefore cannot document my materials with the proper references. This omission, I regret to note, is especially lamentable because I cannot guarantee the credibility of the individuals who communicated with me. My sources seemed respectable enough—they were not "trafficking with dark forces"—but I urge my readers to approach all the material in this work with the proper skepticism.

For readers who may wish to establish personal contact with the Odin Brotherhood, I can provide no certain mechanism. I can affirm, however, that a few members of the Brotherhood are also members of certain Odinist groups that do not shun publicity, so association with "public" Odinist organizations may lead to an encounter with the Brotherhood. A list of non-secret Odinist groups includes the following:

Odinic Rite (England)

Odinist Fellowship (England)

Asatru Alliance (USA)

Asatru Folk Assembly (USA)

The Troth (USA)

Hermandad Asatru Argentina (Argentina)

Sveriges Asatrosamfund (Sweden)

Asatruarfelagid (Iceland)

Comunita Odinista (Italy)

Asatrufellesskapet Bifrost (Norway)

Iberoamerican Asatru Colective (Spain and Chile)

New Zealand Asatru Fellowship (New Zealand)

Germanische Glaubens-Gemeinschaft (Germany)

Regarding the format of this work, I have used the dialogue

form because the poems sacred to all Odinists (the legendary *Eddaic Verses*) used conversational exchange to convey important religious information. There was a negative factor—the *Eddaic* dialogues always end with the death of one of the interlocutors—but I decided to ignore the risk!

The dialogue that resulted is a mosaic made from the fragments of numerous discussions that occurred over several years, and it is not the actual record of one conversation with one individual. Moreover, since most of my sources did not speak English as a first language, the quest for clarity has forced me to use my own words to express their ideas. In all instances, however, I was careful to preserve the fundamental integrity of the message.

Finally, I wish to thank the individuals who made this work possible. In addition to the Odinists who disclosed their secrets to me, I must express my gratitude to Professor Sibylle Herrmann, Dr. James Miller, Dr. John Lorentz, Professor Mary Cummings, and Dr. Anthony Dzik, my learned colleagues at Shawnee State University who generously provided critical evaluations of the text. I must also thank the "Court of Gothar" of the Odinic Rite, Mr. J. D. Holmes and Holmes Publishing Group, World Tree Publications and the Asatru Alliance, Mr. Mogg Morgan, Mr. Gary Stottlemyer, Miss Heather Horner, Miss Taryn L. Malone, Mr. Lee Smith, Miss Sarah Smith, Mr. Matthew Scott, Mr. Stephen A. McNallen, Mr. Valgard Murray, Mr. Robert Gambill, Mr. Anthony Estep, Mr. Ralph Harrison, Mr. Todd Martin, Miss Stephanie V. Schnurbein, Mr. Michael Murray, Miss Casherie Dawn Parker, Mr. Robin Jackson, Mr. Robert Courtney, Miss Heather Elizabeth Cantrell, Mr.

James Arney, Mr. Larry Camp, Mr. Michael Zempter, Miss Tiffany Vincent, Miss Jennifer Robertson, Mr. John Austin, Mr. Stuart McCollum, Mr. William Holmes, Mr. Joseph Varacalli, Mr. Tyler Ferguson, Mr. Michael Neil Reed, Mr. Charles Murray, Miss Valarie Gerlach, Mr. Jeffrey Weaver, Miss Patricia Sissel, Miss Patricia Allen, Mr. Kwak Ho-Sung, Mr. Ragnar Storyteller, Miss Jennifer R. Phillips, Miss Tricia Martineau, Miss Marina Orlova, Miss Sveta Zotava, Miss Melinda Akins, Mr. Eric Goodman, Mr. Alexander Sager, Miss Marianne Griebenow, Miss Jessica Houser, Mr. Timothy Conley, Miss Melissa Hoople, and Miss Brooke Green for their useful comments and suggestions.

Introduction to the Mandrake Edition

This edition—the first for Mandrake of Oxford in England—incorporates small (albeit critical) changes in the text. In all cases, the changes will clarify the message.

As in earlier editions, I have tried to illuminate the unique Odinist perspective on reality. In a time of simplistic creeds and facile explanations, Odinists are men and women who know that space is not as certain, time is not as chronological, and the past is not as dead as most humans believe.

The Dialogue

Odinism and the Mysteries of the Past

AUTHOR: What is Odinism?

THE ODIN BROTHERHOOD: Odinism is an ancient religion that acknowledges the gods by fostering thought, courage, honor, light, and beauty. Older than history, Odinism is all that was called wisdom when the world was new and fresh.

AUTHOR: And what is the Odin Brotherhood?

THE ODIN BROTHERHOOD: The Odin Brotherhood is a secret society for all extraordinary mortals who embrace the principles of Odinism.

AUTHOR: Extraordinary mortals?

THE ODIN BROTHERHOOD: Men and women who possess an epic state of mind.

AUTHOR: When was the Brotherhood established?

THE ODIN BROTHERHOOD: Although Odinism is the primordial religion, the Brotherhood itself is only five centuries old. It was established during the time of our humiliations.

AUTHOR: The time of your "humiliations"?

THE ODIN BROTHERHOOD: The era when Odinism

was the victim of premeditated cruelties. During this dark period, our people were murdered, our temples were annihilated, and our altars were profaned.

AUTHOR: And who persecuted the Odinists?

THE ODIN BROTHERHOOD: Men and women who were black with hate. They called themselves the vassals of Christ, but they were liars.

AUTHOR: And was the use of force effective? Did Odinists betray and abandon their old gods?

THE ODIN BROTHERHOOD: In the end, the Christian terrorism made Odinism stronger.

AUTHOR: Stronger? In what way?

THE ODIN BROTHERHOOD: Purified by violence, Odinism became a religion for the highest form of heroes. From those heroes—the young, the strong, the living—the Odin Brotherhood was born.

AUTHOR: Tell me more about the Brotherhood's origins. In precise terms, how was the movement initiated?

THE ODIN BROTHERHOOD: The Odin Brotherhood was inaugurated in an obscure village built out of gray mud and brown thatch.

AUTHOR: What was the name of the village?

THE ODIN BROTHERHOOD: There are certain facts I must conceal. In the legends, however, the place is called "The-Heart-of-the-White-Darkness."

AUTHOR: And what occurred in this mysterious village?

THE ODIN BROTHERHOOD: The process that would initiate the Brotherhood started in 1418 when an ugly and venomous Christian priest arranged the execution of a young widow.

AUTHOR: What was the widow's name?

THE ODIN BROTHERHOOD: That also must be hidden. In the legends, however, she is called "The-Shrouded-One-of-Odin."

AUTHOR: And why was the woman executed?

THE ODIN BROTHERHOOD: The priest, a man infamous for his bigotry, had seen the young widow honoring the old gods in a remote grotto.

AUTHOR: And "honoring the old gods" was a capital offense?

THE ODIN BROTHERHOOD: That is correct. In the twisted words of the fiendish nonsense that was then called law, death was the punishment for "murmuring heathenish incantations and performing pagan rites."

AUTHOR: So the woman's fate was sealed?

THE ODIN BROTHERHOOD: Yes. The priest did offer to spare her life if she submitted to his carnal lusts, but the young widow scorned his obscene suggestion.

AUTHOR: And did the priest murder her with his own hands?

THE ODIN BROTHERHOOD: No. With eloquent vehemence, the priest inflamed a mob of peasants in the village, and they slaughtered the young widow. In the legends, the mob is called "The-Hundred-Soulless-Authorities."

AUTHOR: And how was the woman killed?

THE ODIN BROTHERHOOD: First they cut her beautiful eyes from her head. Then, with red-hot pincers, they ripped her tongue from her mouth. Finally, they burned her quivering body on a pyre constructed from green wood.

AUTHOR: Why was green wood used?

THE ODIN BROTHERHOOD: It burns slowly and prolongs the agony of the victim.

AUTHOR: The widow's immolation must have been a ghastly spectacle.

THE ODIN BROTHERHOOD: Yes. And her three young children, a boy the legends call "Mocking-Defiance," a girl who is known as "The-Power-of-Innocence," and another boy who is called "Desire-to-Rebel," were forced to watch.

AUTHOR: Was that the priest's idea?

THE ODIN BROTHERHOOD: Yes. And as the children witnessed their mother's sufferings, they were goaded by the priest and his diseased imagination. These were his words:

Hear the hideous bellowing of the harlot who gave you birth? Soon—very soon—she will be groaning in the deepest pit of hell with her counterfeit gods. If you do not become children of the one true church—if you do not learn to kneel, believe, and obey—the devil will one day make you share her pain and her grief.

AUTHOR: And what did the children do?

THE ODIN BROTHERHOOD: Of course, they were not afraid of supernatural terrors.

AUTHOR: Supernatural terrors?

THE ODIN BROTHERHOOD: They did not fear a fictional hell, a scarecrow called the devil, or the other spurious horrors contrived by extinct theologians.

AUTHOR: And why were they not frightened by such things?

THE ODIN BROTHERHOOD: Why fear the webs left by dead spiders?

AUTHOR: So what action did the little ones take? Did they resist the priest?

THE ODIN BROTHERHOOD: No, the children were too clever for that. They realized the priest could not harm their souls, but he could annoy and torment their bodies.

AUTHOR: So what did the children do?

THE ODIN BROTHERHOOD: To save their lives from the Christian menace, the children pretended to embrace the iniquitous fallacies that were being forced upon them.

AUTHOR: And that was an artifice? A tactical maneuver?

THE ODIN BROTHERHOOD: Yes. With their words

they honored the priest's deity—a triune god symbolized as a disagreeable patriarch, a designated scapegoat, and a bland abstraction—but in the depth of their souls they still loved the ancient religion.

AUTHOR: And how did they manifest this love?

THE ODIN BROTHERHOOD: Every winter, the time when death is strong in nature, the children would visit their mother's grave and communicate their affection for the old gods to her.

AUTHOR: Communicate with the dead? How is that possible?

THE ODIN BROTHERHOOD: In Odinist practice, a message inscribed on a lead tablet will reach a dead person if three conditions are met.

AUTHOR: What are those three conditions?

THE ODIN BROTHERHOOD: First, the message must be "reddened" with the fresh blood of a living animal. Second, the lead tablet must be buried at the dead hero's grave in the coldest part of winter. And third, the skull and at least two bones of the deceased must remain intact.

AUTHOR: You mentioned fresh blood. Why is fresh blood necessary?

THE ODIN BROTHERHOOD: Without blood, there is no power. That is the reason animals were cut in half when the biblical Jehovah made his covenant with Abraham.

AUTHOR: Returning to the Odinist practice, will the dead reply to the messages they receive?

THE ODIN BROTHERHOOD: Almost never. In the words of the legends, "the dead can hear but are mute."

AUTHOR: And why are the dead mute?

THE ODIN BROTHERHOOD: Because communicating across the barrier is easier for the living than for the dead.

AUTHOR: But sometimes the dead will reply?

THE ODIN BROTHERHOOD: Indeed. According to our lore, the children received a message from their mother on the third winter after her death.

AUTHOR: Tell me about this necromantic communication.

THE ODIN BROTHERHOOD: In 1421, while standing by their mother's grave, the children suddenly saw a woman dressed in a shroud of white linen.

AUTHOR: Was the woman an apparition? A discarnate entity?

THE ODIN BROTHERHOOD: Visions authenticate nothing. The shrouded woman was physically present at the grave.

AUTHOR: And what happened during the encounter?

THE ODIN BROTHERHOOD: According to the legends, the shrouded woman first made this declaration:

Without the gods, a soul wanders but is not free.

Then, after embracing each child three times, the shrouded woman gave them the three directives.

AUTHOR: And what were these three directives?

THE ODIN BROTHERHOOD: First, the shrouded woman told the children to form a conspiracy of equals—a conspiracy in which every member is a leader.

AUTHOR: What was the second directive?

THE ODIN BROTHERHOOD: The shrouded woman told the children to honor the gods with clandestine rites in deserted places.

AUTHOR: And the third directive?

THE ODIN BROTHERHOOD: She instructed the children to share their knowledge with the few they trusted.

AUTHOR: So the children were to proselytize?

THE ODIN BROTHERHOOD: Before he dies—before he penetrates the mystery of the outer blackness—every Odinist must pass on the wisdom of his secret.

AUTHOR: After the conveyance of the three directives, what happened next?

THE ODIN BROTHERHOOD: The woman made this declaration before returning to the grave:

Heed my words, my children, and the gods of antiquity will be the gods of the future.

AUTHOR: And did the children remember her words?

THE ODIN BROTHERHOOD: Yes. On that very night, they swore a solemn oath cemented with a ceremony of blood. With that oath, the Odin Brotherhood was born.

AUTHOR: And this mysterious fraternity has existed in unbroken succession to the present?

THE ODIN BROTHERHOOD: The Brotherhood bears the teeth marks of Christianity, but it has survived.

The Odin Brotherhood Today and the Heroic Ideal

AUTHOR: What is the status of the Odin Brotherhood in the present age?

THE ODIN BROTHERHOOD: We are a secret aristocracy that penetrates every continent.

AUTHOR: A secret aristocracy?

THE ODIN BROTHERHOOD: A hidden elite. Like the "Hidden Masters" of occult legend, we live unrecognized in the world.

AUTHOR: And what makes an Odinist special?

THE ODIN BROTHERHOOD: An Odinist is a complete man of action. As a member of the invisible army of the gods, he is direct, uncomplicated, and strong.

AUTHOR: Strength seems very important to Odinists.

THE ODIN BROTHERHOOD: Odinism is a Creed of Iron.

AUTHOR: And why is strength so important?

THE ODIN BROTHERHOOD: Because when the gods made man, they made a weapon.

AUTHOR: What kind of weapon?

THE ODIN BROTHERHOOD: One that is hard, and yet supple, dangerous, and yet suave.

AUTHOR: Was not man made from soft clay?

THE ODIN BROTHERHOOD: No. Man was not made from the filth of the earth (as the monotheists claim), and man was not made from carbon, oxygen, and slime (as the materialists claim).

AUTHOR: Then from what substances was man made?

THE ODIN BROTHERHOOD: According to the legends, the gods cut the first man and the first woman from splendid trees. That is the origin of our strength.

AUTHOR: Tell me, what is strength?

THE ODIN BROTHERHOOD: In poetic terms, strength is that which exalts the natural majesty of man.

AUTHOR: And in concrete terms?

THE ODIN BROTHERHOOD: Strength is that which promotes thought and daring.

AUTHOR: And why is strength so important?

THE ODIN BROTHERHOOD: Because it is only by becoming stronger that a man can realize his divinity.

AUTHOR: In other words, through strengi become godlike?

THE ODIN BROTHERHOOD: Yes. And a godlike man— a man who is pure force, inaccessible to any compromise— is called a hero.

AUTHOR: In today's world, where may we find such heroes?

THE ODIN BROTHERHOOD: In any epoch, heroes will be the ones leading the ecstasy of creation or the frenzy of war.

On Polytheism and the Nature of the Gods

AUTHOR: The Odinist ethos is interesting, but let us discuss your gods.

THE ODIN BROTHERHOOD: An excellent idea. A man is what he honors.

AUTHOR: If I may ask this question, why do you honor many gods? Why polytheism?

THE ODIN BROTHERHOOD: Monotheism, the belief in one totalitarian god, is preposterous and absurd. No single, superordinary, ineffable entity controls all realities.

AUTHOR: So the celebrated Judaic-Christian god does not exist? He is merely an occult fiction? A metaphysical figment?

THE ODIN BROTHERHOOD: Those are not my words. The entity called Jehovah (or Yahweh) really does exist—he is a violent god of force and majesty—but he is only one god among many.

AUTHOR: How do you know Jehovah is not unique?

THE ODIN BROTHERHOOD: Even the Old Testament admits the truth. In the first verse of Psalm 82, for example, Jehovah is referred to as a god "among gods."

AUTHOR: But that is only one passage.

THE ODIN BROTHERHOOD: The New Testament, one of the newest of the world's scriptures, also concedes the truth. In I Corinthians, chapter 8, verse 5, Paul of Tarsus writes that "there are many gods and many lords."

AUTHOR: So your polytheism is based on evidence from the Bible?

THE ODIN BROTHERHOOD: Certainly not. Our conviction is based on three foundations.

AUTHOR: And those are?

THE ODIN BROTHERHOOD: First, we appeal to tradition. Man has honored many gods for a thousand centuries. The idea of monotheism, an exaggerated fraud contrived by a malformed Egyptian king, is only thirty centuries old. Thirty centuries! That is only 100 human generations. Such a novelty is rootless, bloodless, meaningless, and unreal.

AUTHOR: And what is the second foundation?

THE ODIN BROTHERHOOD: We appeal to the facts of nature. Observe the universe around you. A universe governed by one supreme deity would possess the maddening simplicity that characterizes any dictatorship, but our cosmos clearly shows no evidence of one will at work. Our universe is characterized by diversity and disorder, and that indicates the universe is molded by many wills and innumerable forces.

AUTHOR: And what is the third foundation for polytheism?

THE ODIN BROTHERHOOD: We appeal to an emotion in our souls: we feel the gods are many.

AUTHOR: Appealing to an emotion is rather irrational.

THE ODIN BROTHERHOOD: True. But Odinists know the irrational can be a source of illumination.

AUTHOR: If we assume that polytheism is correct, how many gods are there?

THE ODIN BROTHERHOOD: Nature—the windowless realm of all existence—is inconceivably complex, and it is filled with nations of gods and tribes of enchanted entities. No mind knows them all.

AUTHOR: So nature literally swarms with gods and godlike beings?

THE ODIN BROTHERHOOD: That is correct. Shintoism of Japan refers to eight million gods, but even that number is far to low.

AUTHOR: Are all gods omnipotent?

THE ODIN BROTHERHOOD: Omnipotence is

humbuggery. In this universe of hazard and adventure, the gods implement their wills through struggle—not fiats.

AUTHOR: The gods seem almost human.

THE ODIN BROTHERHOOD: Of course they are anthropoidal. What is inhuman is not divine.

AUTHOR: But humanoid gods? How is that possible?

THE ODIN BROTHERHOOD: The difference between a god and a man is only one of degree. A god is wiser, stronger, and more beautiful, but a god's fundamental nature is similar to a man's.

AUTHOR: So a god is a species of superhuman?

THE ODIN BROTHERHOOD: That is correct. Amplify all that is great in a man and the result is a god.

AUTHOR: Do Odinists honor all the gods that exist?

THE ODIN BROTHERHOOD: We honor all deities— from Janus of the Romans to Tlazolteotl of the Aztecs—but the movement is especially dedicated to the race of lords depicted in the *Eddaic Verses*.

The Eddaic Verses and the Three Ages of Man

AUTHOR: What are the *Eddaic Verses*?

THE ODIN BROTHERHOOD: The *Eddaic Verses* are ancient poems. Also called "The-Words-of-Power," the *Eddaic Verses* are bold and glowing revelations that describe certain gods that possess the elegance of strength.

AUTHOR: Why are these revelations expressed in verse?

THE ODIN BROTHERHOOD: All transcendental knowledge is expressed in verse. No other medium can effectively convey the instinctual and intellectual forces of gods and "homines noetici."

AUTHOR: "Homines noetici"?

THE ODIN BROTHERHOOD: Thoughtful men.

AUTHOR: And who composed these mysterious *Eddaic Verses*?

THE ODIN BROTHERHOOD: The *Eddaic Verses* were the products of a singular genius.

AUTHOR: And what was the name of that genius?

THE ODIN BROTHERHOOD: In the legends, he is called "Knowledge-Inflamed-By-Imagination." A man of great wisdom, the sages of modern India call him *Vyasa* and claim he still lives somewhere in the mountains of Asia.

AUTHOR: And when did this inspired individual—this "Knowledge-Inflamed-By-Imagination"—compose the poems?

THE ODIN BROTHERHOOD: The *Eddaic Verses* were created during the first age of human history.

AUTHOR: The first age?

THE ODIN BROTHERHOOD: Human history has three periods. The first is called "The-Age-of-Primitive-Freshness."

In this first age, an individual man's chief enemies were predators with hearts of whiteness.

AUTHOR: Who were these predators with hearts of whiteness?

THE ODIN BROTHERHOOD: Wild animals.

AUTHOR: And what is the second age?

THE ODIN BROTHERHOOD: The second age is called the "The-Age-of-Heroic-Gestures." In this period, an individual man's chief enemies were other men.

AUTHOR: And this second age was an age of competition and war?

THE ODIN BROTHERHOOD: Yes. It was the time when men ripened in the sun of adversity.

AUTHOR: And what is the third age?

THE ODIN BROTHERHOOD: The third age is "The-Age-of-Unqualified-Decadence." In this age—the period in which we now live—an individual man's chief enemy is himself.

AUTHOR: And this third age is a period of unequivocal decline?

THE ODIN BROTHERHOOD: Yes. It is the time of self-inflicted wounds.

AUTHOR: Returning to the *Eddaic Verses*, you said these poems were produced during "The-Age-of-Primitive-Freshness"?

THE ODIN BROTHERHOOD: That is correct.

AUTHOR: And what language was used in that ancient period?

THE ODIN BROTHERHOOD: The primordial tongue that is older than time. The prototype of all spoken communication, the primordial tongue is composed only of vowels.

AUTHOR: And is that language still spoken today?

THE ODIN BROTHERHOOD: No contemporary man can speak the primordial tongue. Its beauty has been refracted by the mist of centuries.

AUTHOR: So no one living today can understand the *Eddaic Verses?*

THE ODIN BROTHERHOOD: Not in their original form. But the echoes of antiquity can still be studied in a later version.

AUTHOR: And who recorded this later version?

THE ODIN BROTHERHOOD: A succession of tall, daring, and magnificent warlords who lived in "The-Age-of-Heroic-Gestures."

AUTHOR: And who were these warlords?

THE ODIN BROTHERHOOD: History calls them the Cimmerians, the Scythians, the Sarmatians, and the Vikings. In their eras of greatness, these splendid races were as strong and as clear as mountain rivers.

AUTHOR: And what happened to these splendid races?

THE ODIN BROTHERHOOD: Like all peoples, they eventually lost their innocence and their virility.

AUTHOR: In other words, they became civilized?

THE ODIN BROTHERHOOD: That is correct.

Why Venerate the Odinist Gods?

AUTHOR: Let us return to your gods. Tell me, why single out these Eddaic deities from the countless gods that you say exist?

THE ODIN BROTHERHOOD: To answer that question, I must tell you the story of a young sage named "Innocent-of-Conviction."

AUTHOR: Very well.

THE ODIN BROTHERHOOD: According to an ancient legend, "Innocent-of-Conviction" decided to test the gods to determine which deities deserved the highest honor.

AUTHOR: And how did the sage test the gods?

THE ODIN BROTHERHOOD: By being rude to them.

AUTHOR: Rude?

THE ODIN BROTHERHOOD: Yes. "Innocent-of-Conviction" assaulted the gods by uttering familiar blasphemies.

AUTHOR: An interesting idea.

THE ODIN BROTHERHOOD: Indeed it was. Well, to relate the story, first the sage approached the deity we call "The-Adversary-of-All-Other-Gods." A jealous god, he claims he alone is divine.

AUTHOR: And how did the sage insult this god?

THE ODIN BROTHERHOOD: The sage called him a cruel and ill-tempered desert despot.

AUTHOR: And what happened?

THE ODIN BROTHERHOOD: The deity so addressed erupted into a gruesome display of wrath and anger, and he bullied "Innocent-of-Conviction" into silence.

AUTHOR: The sage was not very brave.

THE ODIN BROTHERHOOD: He was not yet an Odinist.

AUTHOR: Please continue your story.

THE ODIN BROTHERHOOD: Next the sage approached a second deity—the one we call "The-God-Who-Fears-Oblivion-And-Neglect." Pale and dwarfish, he is the god who wants all men to know him and to love him.

AUTHOR: And how did "Innocent-of-Conviction" insult this second god?

THE ODIN BROTHERHOOD: The sage made a reference to the second god's past.

AUTHOR: What did the sage say?

THE ODIN BROTHERHOOD: "Innocent-of-Conviction"

said that any entity who had been born in an animal shed did not smell like a god.

AUTHOR: And how did the second deity react?

THE ODIN BROTHERHOOD: The second deity was displeased and hurt. He lectured the sage—he reprimanded the sage with condescending words—and he concluded his remarks with these words:

You are forgiven. Go, my child, and sin no more!

AUTHOR: This sounds familiar.

THE ODIN BROTHERHOOD: Some deities treat men as children.

AUTHOR: Please continue your story.

THE ODIN BROTHERHOOD: Well, finally the sage sought out the race of lords that we call the Eddaic gods. In a remote mountain citadel, he found them indulging in a feast of pork and wine.

AUTHOR: And how did "Innocent-of-Conviction" insult these Eddaic gods?

THE ODIN BROTHERHOOD: Using a brazen voice, the sage denounced them as false gods who satisfied lusts and procreated monsters.

AUTHOR: And how did the Eddaic gods respond?

THE ODIN BROTHERHOOD: At first there was a moment of silence (the gods were unaccustomed to such bold impieties), but eventually one of the revelers spoke:

Stranger, said the god, *I give you this warning: if I draw my sword, it will not be sheathed again until it has your blood on it.*

AUTHOR: And what did the sage say?

THE ODIN BROTHERHOOD: After a brief pause, he intuited the necessary wisdom. He spoke these words:

Friend, replied the sage, *I have found courage, and a brave man does not fear the wrath of gods.*

AUTHOR: And was the sage punished for his hubris?

THE ODIN BROTHERHOOD: No. To the contrary, the audacity of the sage pleased the Eddaic gods, and all the revelers laughed.

AUTHOR: They laughed?

THE ODIN BROTHERHOOD: Yes. And the Eddaic gods invited "Innocent-of-Conviction" to join their feast, for they admired any man who dared to confront power. Such a man, they declared, was a natural confederate of gods.

AUTHOR: And so the sage had found his answer?

THE ODIN BROTHERHOOD: Indeed. And he had made a discovery as well.

AUTHOR: What discovery?

THE ODIN BROTHERHOOD: Beware of gods who cannot laugh.

AUTHOR: That parable was certainly revealing.

THE ODIN BROTHERHOOD: It was not a parable. According to our legends, the events really occurred during "The-Age-of-Heroic-Gestures."

The Contacts between Men and Gods

AUTHOR: Have many men visited the gods?

THE ODIN BROTHERHOOD: Yes. Usually, however, the gods visit us.

AUTHOR: Do you mean that literally?

THE ODIN BROTHERHOOD: Of course. Some deities are occasional interlopers in the world of men, but the Eddaic gods are different. The Eddaic gods constantly wander across the face of the Earth.

AUTHOR: And do your gods visit all nations?

THE ODIN BROTHERHOOD: In the eyes of gods, there are no chosen peoples and no master races. Higher men and higher women—the elite from all nations—share the proximity of the gods.

AUTHOR: And why do the Eddaic gods visit the world of men? Do they have a purpose?

THE ODIN BROTHERHOOD: The world of men is more exciting than the world of the gods, so deities like to come here for amusement and adventure.

AUTHOR: So the gods like to see, to hear, and to feel the experiences of this world?

THE ODIN BROTHERHOOD: That is correct.

AUTHOR: And do the gods also come here for more serious purposes?

THE ODIN BROTHERHOOD: Yes. Sometimes they visit the world of men in the interest of knowledge.

AUTHOR: You mean, they come to Earth to spread their faith?

THE ODIN BROTHERHOOD: No. The gods come here to learn.

AUTHOR: Learn? The gods can learn from men? But are not the gods all-knowing and all-wise?

THE ODIN BROTHERHOOD: No god is all-knowing and all-wise.

AUTHOR: Even the Christian god?

THE ODIN BROTHERHOOD: Omnisciency is not possible. An omniscient god would suffocate in his own wisdom.

AUTHOR: Let us return to the subject of godly visits. Tell me, if the gods visit our world often, why have I never seen one?

THE ODIN BROTHERHOOD: In fact, you may have encountered gods or goddesses and not recognized them.

AUTHOR: Explain.

THE ODIN BROTHERHOOD: The gods do not need theatrics to impress mortals: they do not have to communicate through angelic thralls or burning bushes. Normally, their visits are far more discreet, and they can pass unnoticed in a crowd of humanity.

AUTHOR: Can you provide examples?

THE ODIN BROTHERHOOD: Yes. If, while enjoying the winter, you encounter a wise and mysterious stranger who has a hood drawn low over his face—that could be a god. If, while walking down a city street, you encounter a woman who is a visual work of art—that could be a goddess.

AUTHOR: Does a given god or a goddess always appear in the same form?

THE ODIN BROTHERHOOD: No. The deities often manufacture unreality.

AUTHOR: Manufacture unreality?

THE ODIN BROTHERHOOD: They create illusions, and they appear as they are not. Thus, one god actually visited Earth disguised as a man with a long nose and a bald pate.

AUTHOR: Humorous. But, if deities are masters of disguise, how can I determine if I have met a god?

THE ODIN BROTHERHOOD: You will know you are in the presence of a god when you sense something powerful, something exceptional, something human.

AUTHOR: Are there more precise indications?

THE ODIN BROTHERHOOD: Yes. According to the legends, a god will cast a light shadow but not a dark shadow.

AUTHOR: Explain.

THE ODIN BROTHERHOOD: A light shadow is a reflection in a mirror. A dark shadow is the silhouette that is cast in sunlight.

AUTHOR: And a god will not cast this silhouette?

THE ODIN BROTHERHOOD: That is correct.

AUTHOR: If that is true, how can a god hide his identity? Having no dark shadow is an anomaly that would be readily noticed.

THE ODIN BROTHERHOOD: To conceal themselves in the world of men, the gods normally appear only at night or at noon.

AUTHOR: Noon?

THE ODIN BROTHERHOOD: In the vertical beams of the midday sun, there are no dark shadows.

AUTHOR: When the Eddaic gods visit Earth, from where do they come?

THE ODIN BROTHERHOOD: They come from the illustrious city of Asgard.

AUTHOR: Asgard?

THE ODIN BROTHERHOOD: The enclave of the Eddaic deities in the reality of the gods.

AUTHOR: Where is this "reality of the gods"? Is it in a parallel universe? Another dimension? Another plane of existence?

THE ODIN BROTHERHOOD: I will say only this: nature has hidden corridors that most men have only seen in their dreams. The reality of the gods exists in one of those corridors.

AUTHOR: And how do the Eddaic deities reach Earth from Asgard?

THE ODIN BROTHERHOOD: The reality of the gods has a mysterious door that opens in the world of men.

AUTHOR: A door?

THE ODIN BROTHERHOOD: Yes. In nature, the reality of the gods intersects the reality of men. When the two realities are perpendicular, the mysterious door is formed.

AUTHOR: Where is this aperture located?

THE ODIN BROTHERHOOD: When it appears, it is on the frontier between the visible and the invisible.

AUTHOR: Can you be more specific?

THE ODIN BROTHERHOOD: No—for the door is never in the same place.

AUTHOR: Explain.

THE ODIN BROTHERHOOD: The door is constantly in motion. On one occasion it may appear on a mountain summit—on another occasion it may appear in the depths of the sea.

AUTHOR: If the door ambulates, how can it be found?

THE ODIN BROTHERHOOD: To locate the door, look for "The-Bridge-of-Opaque-Colors."

AUTHOR: "The-Bridge-of-Opaque-Colors"?

THE ODIN BROTHERHOOD: The rainbow that is saturated with beauty.

The God Odin and His Mysteries

AUTHOR: Let us return to your gods. So far, we have discussed your gods in general. Now tell me about individual deities.

THE ODIN BROTHERHOOD: We can begin with Odin, the "All-Father."

AUTHOR: Why is he called "All-Father"?

THE ODIN BROTHERHOOD: Because Odin, the inscrutable one, the god who speaks in poetry, wields paternal authority in Asgard.

AUTHOR: As "All-Father," is Odin the creator of nature?

THE ODIN BROTHERHOOD: Nature, in its various forms, has always existed. No god created it.

AUTHOR: So our universe has no beginning and no end?

THE ODIN BROTHERHOOD: In the infinitude that is nature, innumerable universes are successively produced and destroyed by periodic convulsions. Our universe is only one of many. Like all such universes, ours was formed from the wreckage of the previous cosmos, and the next universe will be formed from the ruins of our cosmos.

AUTHOR: I see. So nature goes through an almost biological process of birth, death, and rebirth—composition, decomposition, recomposition?

THE ODIN BROTHERHOOD: In rough form, you have articulated a great truth.

AUTHOR: And this process is independent of any god?

THE ODIN BROTHERHOOD: The gods did not create nature. To the contrary, nature is a matrix that gives birth to gods.

AUTHOR: So the gods are the products of a genesis and not the initiators of it?

THE ODIN BROTHERHOOD: Exactly. Nature herself is the womb of pantheons.

AUTHOR: Well, if Odin is not the creator, why does he have authority among the gods?

THE ODIN BROTHERHOOD: Because he is wise. Odin thinks in terms of centuries, and he knows deep, mysterious, and unfathomable things.

AUTHOR: And how did Odin gain such wisdom?

THE ODIN BROTHERHOOD: Through struggle.

AUTHOR: Can you be more precise?

THE ODIN BROTHERHOOD: According to the legends, Odin sacrificed one of his eyes to drink a draft of wisdom.

AUTHOR: Did he do anything else?

THE ODIN BROTHERHOOD: Odin endured horrible agonies to discover the knowledge of the runes.

AUTHOR: What are the runes?

THE ODIN BROTHERHOOD: Occult potencies.

AUTHOR: And these are useful?

THE ODIN BROTHERHOOD: With the runes, the adept can learn from the past and communicate with the future. He can also heal all diseases, blunt all weapons, break all fetters, quench all fires, calm all storms, end all hatreds, and win all loves.

AUTHOR: Interesting claims. How can these runes perform such wonders?

THE ODIN BROTHERHOOD: The runes are mystic passwords that unleash the power of matter, energy, and thought.

AUTHOR: Can you elaborate?

THE ODIN BROTHERHOOD: I can say no more. There are certain secrets that must not be revealed.

AUTHOR: You can add nothing else?

THE ODIN BROTHERHOOD: Only this: if you knew the secret of the runes, the knowledge would surprise and terrify.

AUTHOR: Returning to Odin, what agonies did the god

suffer to discover the "occult potencies" that are called runes?

THE ODIN BROTHERHOOD: The legends are rather vague here, but listen to the words of Odin from the *Eddaic Verses*, the ancient words of power:

> *I know that I hung*
> *On the windswept tree*
> *For nine nights long,*
> *Wounded by a spear*
> *And consecrated to Odin*
> *Myself to myself,*
> *On the mighty tree*
> *Of which no man knows*
> *From what root it springs.*
> *No one refreshed me*
> *With drink or bread;*
> *I looked downward*
> *And took up the runes,*
> *Shrieking I took them,*
> *Then I fell to the ground.*

AUTHOR: The words of power are as obscure as they are suggestive. What do they mean?

THE ODIN BROTHERHOOD: To seize the runes, Odin mounted a gallows called "The-World-Tree-of-Knowledge." Purified by suffering, the god sacrificed himself to himself.

AUTHOR: In a fashion, the sufferings of Odin evoke the passion of Christ.

THE ODIN BROTHERHOOD: Not surprisingly. Gods—

like the prophets and the shamans who live in the world of men—understand that pain can be a source of illumination.

AUTHOR: Can knowledge be found without pain?

THE ODIN BROTHERHOOD: Of course. In fact, Odin also seeks wisdom through simple travel. He often visits the world of men, and that is the reason he is called the god of countless names.

AUTHOR: Are you suggesting that every time Odin visited a different nation he was given a different appellation?

THE ODIN BROTHERHOOD: Yes. Called Rudra, Hermes, and Wotan, Odin bears many names. He is also called "Hooded-One," "Much-Loved," "Third-One," "Thin-One," "One-Who-Blinds-With-Death," "High-One," "Changeable-One," "One-Who-Guesses-Right," "Glad-of-War," "God-of-the-Spear," "One-Whose-Eye-Deceives-Him," "Flame-Eyed-One," "Worker-of-Destruction," "Bringer-of-Ecstasy," "Very-Wise-One," "Long-Bearded-One," "Father-of-Victory," "Cargo-God," "God-of-Wishes," "Just-As-High," "Wand-Bearer," "Gray-Bearded-One," "Terrible-One," "Wanderer," and "Father-of-the-Slain."

AUTHOR: An impressive list of names.

THE ODIN BROTHERHOOD: And each one is a skeleton key to a special mystery.

AUTHOR: Can you explain those mysteries?

THE ODIN BROTHERHOOD: Mysteries should not be explained—they should be experienced. That is the way of Odin.

The Goddess Frigg and the Rite of Marriage

AUTHOR: Let us discuss some of the other deities honored by the Brotherhood.

THE ODIN BROTHERHOOD: Very well. Another entity we honor is a goddess named Frigg. As the wife of Odin, Frigg is the patroness of marriage.

AUTHOR: Is marriage important to Odinists?

THE ODIN BROTHERHOOD: Without marriage, the procreative act cannot be a sacrament. And when there are no commitments—no nuptial commitments—men and women fall into the bottomless pit of erotic anarchy.

AUTHOR: Do Odinists have a special marriage ceremony?

THE ODIN BROTHERHOOD: Yes. It is called "The-Beatitude-of-Frigg."

AUTHOR: Please describe it for me.

THE ODIN BROTHERHOOD: "The-Beatitude-of-Frigg" begins with a great feast with friends and relatives.

AUTHOR: How long does this feast last?

THE ODIN BROTHERHOOD: Until twilight. Then the couple to be married retire to the bridal chamber.

AUTHOR: And what happens when they reach the bridal chamber?

THE ODIN BROTHERHOOD: To consecrate the nuptial ceremony, the bride and groom hold hands and together they speak these words:

Love is a spark that leaps between our souls. Come! Let us rise to the light!

Next, uniting all the senses, the bride and groom embrace once. Each then speaks these words to the other:

On this night of special ecstasy, I give you my innocence. As long as I live, I will give you my love.

Finally, the bride and the groom kiss once, and together they complete the rite with this declaration:

Bone to bone, blood to blood, flesh to flesh. Moved by the desire to create, from this hour our bodies are one.

AUTHOR: Powerful words.

THE ODIN BROTHERHOOD: Yes. And our legends teach that they were first spoken by Frigg and her husband.

The God Thor, the Nemesis of Titans

AUTHOR: Let us discuss another one of your deities.

THE ODIN BROTHERHOOD: Another significant god is Thor, "The-Lord-of-the-Hammer."

AUTHOR: Why is this Thor called "The-Lord-of-the-Hammer"?

THE ODIN BROTHERHOOD: Because Thor possesses a tool that breaks chains and crushes enemies—an enchanted mallet that strikes with the roar of thunder and the flash of lightning.

AUTHOR: What kind of god is Thor?

THE ODIN BROTHERHOOD: Thor is one of the most popular of our deities. Known as the "the strong one of the gods," Thor is the son of Odin and the father of one daughter, Thrud (strength), and two sons, Magni (colossal might) and Modi (fierce courage).

AUTHOR: Why is Thor so popular?

THE ODIN BROTHERHOOD: Three reasons. First, Thor is popular because he is the favorite of adventurers.

AUTHOR: And what is an adventurer?

THE ODIN BROTHERHOOD: Someone who accomplishes great deeds in the spirit of play.

AUTHOR: And the second reason?

THE ODIN BROTHERHOOD: Thor is popular because he is the friend of heroes.

AUTHOR: And how does Thor recognize a hero?

THE ODIN BROTHERHOOD: In any combat, the hero is the one who renounces advantages.

AUTHOR: And what is the third reason?

THE ODIN BROTHERHOOD: Thor is popular because his kindness has no visible limits.

AUTHOR: Benevolence is important to Odinists?

THE ODIN BROTHERHOOD: Of course. Without kindness, a man cannot be human. That is the teaching of Thor.

AUTHOR: Tell me more about Thor, "The-Lord-of-the-Hammer."

THE ODIN BROTHERHOOD: As the strongest of the gods, Thor leads the struggle against the titans.

AUTHOR: Who are the titans?

THE ODIN BROTHERHOOD: Also called the giants, Thor's foes are creatures who possess vast power and profound wisdom. Fiercely independent—they hate to be enclosed or dominated—the giants are older than the gods and are hostile to them.

AUTHOR: Older than the gods?

THE ODIN BROTHERHOOD: The titans are the elder ones. They are the offspring of Ymir, the "first of the living" in our universe.

AUTHOR: And from where did Ymir come?

THE ODIN BROTHERHOOD: In the matrix that is time, Ymir (the name means "the roarer") emerged from the chaos of ice and fire.

AUTHOR: The chaos of ice and fire?

THE ODIN BROTHERHOOD: The ruins of the universe that preceded our own.

AUTHOR: And where is this Ymir now?

THE ODIN BROTHERHOOD: Ymir is dead, but his corpse is a part of nature and the titans he engendered live on.

AUTHOR: And where do Ymir's offspring live?

THE ODIN BROTHERHOOD: There are two kinds of titans who do combat with Thor. Those who are called frost giants live in a place of endless night and immaculate coldness.

AUTHOR: And where does the second type live?

THE ODIN BROTHERHOOD: The other type of titans—those who are called fire giants—live in a brimstone abyss at the edge of an unknown plateau.

AUTHOR: Can these titan realms be reached from the reality of men?

THE ODIN BROTHERHOOD: No. They exist in oblique corridors.

AUTHOR: So the titan realms are inaccessible?

THE ODIN BROTHERHOOD: To journey to the realms of Thor's enemies, one has to create an aperture with the brute power.

AUTHOR: And who possesses the necessary force?

THE ODIN BROTHERHOOD: The hero can cut a swath of destruction through any barrier. That is the teaching of Thor.

The Goddess Sif, the Mischief of Loki, and the Skill of the Rock Dwarfs

AUTHOR: Tell me about another Eddaic deity.

THE ODIN BROTHERHOOD: There is the goddess named Sif. The wife of Thor, Sif is renowned throughout all worlds for a misfortune she once suffered.

AUTHOR: What misfortune?

THE ODIN BROTHERHOOD: Her exquisite long hair was destroyed by the one named Loki. A frost giant by birth, Loki is the master of stealth, cunning, and guile.

AUTHOR: And why did this frost giant—this one named Loki—do such a deed?

THE ODIN BROTHERHOOD: Because Loki is a prankster and mischief is his delight.

AUTHOR: Is Loki the Odinist devil?

THE ODIN BROTHERHOOD: In the eyes of Odinists, there are no devils. Even Lucifer—the vile Archfiend in Christian mythology—is in fact a fallen god.

AUTHOR: Returning to Sif, did her hair eventually grow back?

THE ODIN BROTHERHOOD: No. But threatened by Sif's husband, Loki replaced the lost hair of the goddess with enchanted tresses.

AUTHOR: Enchanted tresses?

THE ODIN BROTHERHOOD: Wondrous strands of pure gold that grew as real hair grows.

AUTHOR: And did Loki make this golden hair himself?

THE ODIN BROTHERHOOD: No. At his request, it was forged by the rock dwarfs.

AUTHOR: Rock dwarfs?

THE ODIN BROTHERHOOD: Superb craftsmen who are the masters of created things.

AUTHOR: Describe these rock dwarfs.

THE ODIN BROTHERHOOD: The masters of dexterity are tiny creatures with putty-colored skin, large, frog-like eyes, and small, turned-up noses.

AUTHOR: And where do they live?

THE ODIN BROTHERHOOD: The makers of Sif's hair live in the crust of the Earth.

AUTHOR: Directly in the crust?

THE ODIN BROTHERHOOD: Yes. The rock dwarfs can pass through solid stone as easily as a shark swims through water or a hawk flies through air.

AUTHOR: And do these rock dwarfs ever visit our surface world?

THE ODIN BROTHERHOOD: Rock dwarfs rarely visit our world—the legends say the power of sunlight turns them into stone—but sometimes they are accidently seen in the darkness of night.

AUTHOR: And who usually sees the rock dwarfs?

THE ODIN BROTHERHOOD: Human females.

AUTHOR: Why females?

THE ODIN BROTHERHOOD: The makers of Sif's hair are intoxicated by beauty, and they like to spy on charming maidens.

AUTHOR: Do they fall in love with such females?

THE ODIN BROTHERHOOD: Of course.

AUTHOR: And is their love returned?

THE ODIN BROTHERHOOD: Sadly, no rock dwarf is ever successful in love.

The God Heimdall and "The-Sojourn-of-the-Brave"

AUTHOR: Returning to the gods, tell me about another Eddaic deity.

THE ODIN BROTHERHOOD: Another significant member of the race of lords is Heimdall the Vigilant.

AUTHOR: Why is Heimdall important?

THE ODIN BROTHERHOOD: Heimdall is the indefatigable guardian of the two holy places.

AUTHOR: What are the two holy places?

THE ODIN BROTHERHOOD: The first is "The-Bridge-of-Opaque-Colors" that leads to Asgard.

AUTHOR: And the second?

THE ODIN BROTHERHOOD: The initiation ritual that leads to the Odin Brotherhood.

AUTHOR: Your secret society has an initiation ritual?

THE ODIN BROTHERHOOD: Yes. And to experience the ritual is to become a member of the Brotherhood.

AUTHOR: May anyone experience this ritual?

THE ODIN BROTHERHOOD: In theory, the answer is yes.

AUTHOR: But how do you exclude the unworthy?

THE ODIN BROTHERHOOD: According to the wisdom of Heimdall, the unworthy exclude themselves.

AUTHOR: Explain.

THE ODIN BROTHERHOOD: The Brotherhood demands much from its members and promises nothing in return. Such conditions attract the great and repel all who are small, cowardly, and smug.

AUTHOR: And why is that true?

THE ODIN BROTHERHOOD: Because only higher men and women join a legion of honor for honor's sake.

AUTHOR: And the Odin Brotherhood is a legion of honor?

THE ODIN BROTHERHOOD: That is the teaching of Heimdall.

AUTHOR: Describe your initiation ritual.

THE ODIN BROTHERHOOD: Presided over by Heimdall, the ritual is a solemn and ancient ceremony cemented with blood. In the legends, it is known as "The-Sojourn-of-the-Brave."

AUTHOR: And why is the rite called "The -Sojourn-of-the-Brave"?

THE ODIN BROTHERHOOD: Because the neophyte (the person who is consecrated) experiences the symbolism of his own violent death.

AUTHOR: How does the "Sojourn" begin?

THE ODIN BROTHERHOOD: The journey begins with "The-Meeting-of-Dreams."

AUTHOR: What is that?

THE ODIN BROTHERHOOD: "The-Meeting-of-Dreams" is a special vision encountered during sleep. In the vision, the neophyte is called to the Brotherhood.

AUTHOR: And who receives such a vision?

THE ODIN BROTHERHOOD: A man or a woman who is first prepared by Heimdall.

AUTHOR: Explain.

THE ODIN BROTHERHOOD: The person called will meet a special messenger from Heimdall. The fantastic visitor—a god or a human envoy from the gods—will point the way to the Brotherhood.

AUTHOR: And how were you "prepared"?

THE ODIN BROTHERHOOD: Many years ago, a young woman named "Unashamed-Beauty" told me about the movement. Later, I encountered the vision in my dreams.

AUTHOR: Describe the vision. What does the neophyte see?

THE ODIN BROTHERHOOD: The vision may take many forms. In my own meeting of dreams, I saw three men of bronze, and they spoke to me.

AUTHOR: What did they say?

THE ODIN BROTHERHOOD: First they said their names were "Courage," "Audacity," and "Revolt." Then, speaking with one voice, they made this declaration:

Awake! There is distance to conquer and space to shape!

AUTHOR: And what did you do?

THE ODIN BROTHERHOOD: In the dream I was confused, but all became clear when the men of bronze uttered these words:

Like a god you must live, and like a god you must die!

AUTHOR: And that was your calling?

THE ODIN BROTHERHOOD: Yes. And I answered the summons of Heimdall.

AUTHOR: Let us continue. After the vision—after the encounter with the dream—what must the neophyte do?

THE ODIN BROTHERHOOD: The neophyte must wait for the Summer Solstice or the Winter Solstice. In the northern hemisphere, these occur on June 22 and December 22 respectively.

AUTHOR: What is the significance of the solstices? Why are those times of the year special?

THE ODIN BROTHERHOOD: During the solstices, there are fractures in the reality of the gods. These fractures cause divine forces to seep into the world of men.

AUTHOR: I understand. Well, let us assume it is the time of one of the solstices. What action must the neophyte take?

THE ODIN BROTHERHOOD: The neophyte must gather wood from a tree that has been struck by lightning.

AUTHOR: Why a special tree?

THE ODIN BROTHERHOOD: In ancient legends, lightning emanates from the gods.

AUTHOR: I understand. Please continue.

THE ODIN BROTHERHOOD: The neophyte must forge a new dagger from old materials.

AUTHOR: Why a dagger?

THE ODIN BROTHERHOOD: The weapon that cuts is nobler than the weapon that strikes or the weapon that burns.

AUTHOR: After the dagger is forged, what is the next step?

THE ODIN BROTHERHOOD: The neophyte must seek absolute solitude on a mountain in the wilderness. For three nights and three days he must not see a human face or hear a human voice.

AUTHOR: While on the mountain, does the initiate live in the open?

THE ODIN BROTHERHOOD: He may. Normally, however, the neophyte will stay in an isolated shelter or dwelling.

AUTHOR: Tell me, what is the significance of the mountain location?

THE ODIN BROTHERHOOD: Some men become terrified and dizzy at great heights. According to an old legend, it is the proximity of the gods at great heights that makes some people afraid.

AUTHOR: So the initiate goes up the mountain to be closer to his gods?

THE ODIN BROTHERHOOD: Correct.

AUTHOR: During the three nights and three days of solitude on the mountain, what should the initiate do?

THE ODIN BROTHERHOOD: Alone with his thoughts, he must survive on a diet of bread and ice.

AUTHOR: In other words, the initiate purges himself by fasting?

THE ODIN BROTHERHOOD: Yes. No man can find illumination when he is swollen with food and sodden with drink.

AUTHOR: And why bread and ice? Why those substances?

THE ODIN BROTHERHOOD: They are the foods of Heimdall. The neophyte will gain strength from the bread and will see the future in the translucent ice.

AUTHOR: I understand. Please continue. What occurs after the fast of three days and three nights?

THE ODIN BROTHERHOOD: The neophyte now begins the most hallowed part of the ritual. He must bathe in clear water—he must dress himself in a shroud that is pure and white—and he must build a fire from the wood he has gathered.

AUTHOR: Does the flame have special significance?

THE ODIN BROTHERHOOD: According to our traditions, fire is alive: it experiences birth and death, growth and motion, and it must be fed.

AUTHOR: So fire is an entity?

THE ODIN BROTHERHOOD: Yes. Pure and naked, fire is a luminous entity that communicates with the gods.

AUTHOR: Please continue. What happens after the fire is prepared?

THE ODIN BROTHERHOOD: The neophyte must stand before the flame and utter the ancient words:

In the name of holy violence, necessary violence!

Then, using the dagger he has made, the male neophyte must

make three incisions on his chest. The scars are called "The-Marks-of-Joy."

AUTHOR: Shedding blood in a religious initiation ceremony seems rather savage.

THE ODIN BROTHERHOOD: Blood rites are found in other religions. When pious Jews initiate a male into their group, for example, they circumcise human flesh. In their lore, this is called "the sign of the covenant."

AUTHOR: Returning to the Odinist practice, you specifically noted that a *male* neophyte cuts himself. What does the female initiate do? Does she make scars on her chest?

THE ODIN BROTHERHOOD: The female's breasts—the last and most beautiful embellishment she receives in life—must not be disfigured. Instead, the woman makes three small incisions on the tip of her right index finger.

AUTHOR: So when drawn from a lovely woman's body, a small offering of blood is sufficient?

THE ODIN BROTHERHOOD: That is the teaching of Heimdall.

AUTHOR: Once the lesions are made—once the flesh is slashed—what happens next?

THE ODIN BROTHERHOOD: Using the point of the dagger, the neophyte must extract part of his soul from each of the three wounds.

AUTHOR: Explain.

THE ODIN BROTHERHOOD: Odinists believe that the soul is in the blood. Based on this belief, he who extracts some of his blood is extracting part of his soul.

AUTHOR: And he who offers part of his soul is undergoing a symbolic death?

THE ODIN BROTHERHOOD: That is correct.

AUTHOR: What happens next?

THE ODIN BROTHERHOOD: The neophyte, after staining the dagger from all three wounds, must now offer it to the gods of Asgard.

AUTHOR: How is that accomplished?

THE ODIN BROTHERHOOD: The neophyte penetrates the flame three times with the dagger stained with his own blood. As he does so, he solemnly declares:

> *With this blood, I devote, hallow, and sanctify my soul to the gods who live.*

Then the neophyte solemnly repeats the names of all the gods of the Brotherhood. Their names are Balder, Bragi, Bur, Buri, Eir, Forseti, Frey, Freyja, Frigg, Fulla, Gefjon, Gna, Heimdall, Hermod, Hlin, Hod, Hoenir, Idun, Jord, Kvasir, Lodur, Lofn, Loki, Magni, Meili, Mimir, Modi, Nanna, Njord, Odin, Ran, Rind, Saga, Sif, Sigyn, Sjofn, Skadi, Snotra, Syn, Thor, Thrud, Tyr, Ull, Vali, Var, Vidar, Vili, Ve, and Vor.

AUTHOR: Your list includes Loki, the "mischief-maker." Is he not a frost giant by birth?

THE ODIN BROTHERHOOD: Before this world ends, Loki lives in Asgard. Since roguish Loki represents enjoyment without responsibility—since he is a playful flash of light from the darkness—the gods welcome his comradeship.

AUTHOR: Returning to the "Sojourn-of-the-Brave," what must the neophyte do after he has named all the gods?

THE ODIN BROTHERHOOD: The neophyte closes the rite by extinguishing the flame and making the final utterance.

AUTHOR: And what is the final utterance?

THE ODIN BROTHERHOOD: The neophyte, reaching into the depths of his being, will speak these words:

> *The rite is finished. Let my violent thrust into the future begin!*

The God Bragi, the Holy Words, and the Seasonal Rites

AUTHOR: Heimdall and his rite certainly possess the thrill of mystery.

THE ODIN BROTHERHOOD: Indeed he does. And another deity, the god named Bragi, also is a patron of ritual arcana.

AUTHOR: In what way?

THE ODIN BROTHERHOOD: Bragi, a son of Odin and the husband of a goddess named Idun, is the god of the eloquent words. When Odinists call upon their gods, they do so under the patronage of Bragi.

AUTHOR: You mean, Bragi is the Odinist god of prayer?

THE ODIN BROTHERHOOD: Bragi is the god of sacred communications. The word "prayer"—which originally meant "to beg"— is taboo to Odinists.

AUTHOR: Tell me, why does an Odinist address his gods?

THE ODIN BROTHERHOOD: Because he is one of the "theophiloi"—the friends of gods.

AUTHOR: And a man should communicate with his friends?

THE ODIN BROTHERHOOD: That is correct.

AUTHOR: When he calls upon his gods, does the Odinist ask for divine guidance?

THE ODIN BROTHERHOOD: Never. A man who follows a leader is a man who thinks by proxy.

AUTHOR: In his sacred communications, does an Odinist ever ask for divine assistance?

THE ODIN BROTHERHOOD: No Odinist ever asks for help. Self-reliant, he would rather steal than accept charity.

AUTHOR: When he calls upon his gods, does an Odinist ever confess his sins in a spirit of contrition?

THE ODIN BROTHERHOOD: No. Contrition—a totem of decadence—is alien to Odinism.

AUTHOR: Why do Odinists scorn repentance?

THE ODIN BROTHERHOOD: Because repentance is an act of cowardice. Remember, only the terrorized repent.

AUTHOR: But what if a man has dishonored himself?

THE ODIN BROTHERHOOD: With fortitude, the hero accepts the consequences of his shameful action. With invincible strength, he resolves not to repeat the error.

AUTHOR: When an Odinist utters the "holy words"—when he addresses his friends the gods—does he need a priest?

THE ODIN BROTHERHOOD: Every Odinist is a priest and an apostle.

AUTHOR: Do Odinists use temples?

THE ODIN BROTHERHOOD: The gods may be honored anywhere as long as the three rules are followed.

AUTHOR: What are the three rules?

THE ODIN BROTHERHOOD: When communicating with gods, all strangers must be excluded, all words must be whispered, and all abominations must be avoided.

AUTHOR: Abominations?

THE ODIN BROTHERHOOD: Promiscuity and assassination.

AUTHOR: When the gods are honored, is a special ceremony used?

THE ODIN BROTHERHOOD: Yes. It is called "The-Rite-of-Bragi."

AUTHOR: When is this rite performed?

THE ODIN BROTHERHOOD: In the course of a year, "The-Rite-of-Bragi" is celebrated on three sacred festivals.

AUTHOR: And what are these festivals?

THE ODIN BROTHERHOOD: The first is called "The-Night-of-Joy." Held in honor of the goddesses, the "The-Night-of-Joy" occurs on the eve of the summer solstice.

AUTHOR: Why is this first festival called "The-Night-of-Joy"?

THE ODIN BROTHERHOOD: Because the summer solstice celebration of "The-Rite-of-Bragi" includes feasting, jocularity, and frivolity.

AUTHOR: What is the second festival?

THE ODIN BROTHERHOOD: The second is called "The-Night-of-Courage." Held in honor of all the Odinists who have died, "The-Night-of-Courage" occurs on October 31.

AUTHOR: Why October 31?

THE ODIN BROTHERHOOD: In the old calendar, October 31 marks the beginning of winter—the time when death is strong in nature.

AUTHOR: Why is the second festival called "The-Night-of-Courage"?

THE ODIN BROTHERHOOD: Because the October 31 celebration of "The-Rite-of-Bragi" includes a tribute to the heroes of the past.

AUTHOR: Heroes of the past?

THE ODIN BROTHERHOOD: Men and women who neither lived quietly nor died quietly.

AUTHOR: And what is the third festival?

THE ODIN BROTHERHOOD: The third is called "The-Night-of-Generosity." Held in honor of the gods, "The-Night-of-Generosity" occurs on the eve of the Winter Solstice.

AUTHOR: Why is the third festival called "The-Night-of-Generosity"?

THE ODIN BROTHERHOOD: Because the Winter Solstice celebration of "The-Rite-of-Bragi" includes the bestowal of gifts.

AUTHOR: What kind of gifts?

THE ODIN BROTHERHOOD: During the Winter Solstice, every Odinist gives the world something great and something beautiful.

AUTHOR: On the matter of "The-Rite-of-Bragi," could you provide details of the ritual?

THE ODIN BROTHERHOOD: Yes. First, the celebrant ritually purifies himself by washing his body and dressing in a shroud that is pure and white. Then he must wait for the darkness of night.

AUTHOR: Using the darkness of night is a practice that began during the persecution, the time of your "humiliations"?

THE ODIN BROTHERHOOD: That is correct.

AUTHOR: Please continue.

THE ODIN BROTHERHOOD: After the descent of the sun, the celebrant positions himself before a luminous object.

AUTHOR: A flame?

THE ODIN BROTHERHOOD: Any source of light, from a candle to the starfire in the sky.

AUTHOR: Please continue.

THE ODIN BROTHERHOOD: The celebrant stands erect with his eyes and arms raised and declares these words:

A man without gods has a desert in his heart.

AUTHOR: The celebrant does not kneel?

THE ODIN BROTHERHOOD: Kneeling is for slaves.

AUTHOR: Humility has no place in Odinism?

THE ODIN BROTHERHOOD: Odinism is the enemy of all abjection.

AUTHOR: Returning to "The-Rite-of-Bragi," what does the celebrant do after he has made his declaration?

THE ODIN BROTHERHOOD: For many heartbeats, the celebrant moves through time without moving through space.

AUTHOR: Explain.

THE ODIN BROTHERHOOD: The celebrant stands motionless. When a man is still, the poets say he is moving through time without moving through space.

AUTHOR: I see. Please continue.

THE ODIN BROTHERHOOD: Next, the celebrant touches all the gods and goddesses of Asgard.

AUTHOR: Touches? How does a man touch a god?

THE ODIN BROTHERHOOD: By naming all the deities one by one.

AUTHOR: I am not certain I understand.

THE ODIN BROTHERHOOD: According to the ancients, naming is a kind of touching, for the name is a part of the thing.

AUTHOR: I see. And what happens next?

THE ODIN BROTHERHOOD: After touching all the gods and goddesses, the celebrant advances to the final and most mystical part of "The-Rite-of-Bragi."

AUTHOR: Does the final part of the rite have a special name?

THE ODIN BROTHERHOOD: Yes. It is called "The-Glimpse-of-Extraordinary-Beauty."

AUTHOR: And what does this final procedure involve?

THE ODIN BROTHERHOOD: Standing before a luminous object, the celebrant must first select one god or one goddess from our sacred pantheon. Then—in the cauldron of thought—in the crucible that men call imagination—the celebrant must visualize himself as the deity he has selected.

AUTHOR: If the visualization is successful, what will occur?

THE ODIN BROTHERHOOD: If the celebrant achieves his vision—if he literally sees himself as one of the race of lords—he will experience "The-Glimpse-of-Extraordinary-Beauty."

AUTHOR: And can you describe the experience?

THE ODIN BROTHERHOOD: I will say only this: when a man enjoys "The-Glimpse-of-Extraordinary-Beauty," he is enveloped and penetrated by the thoughts of a god.

AUTHOR: How is such a thing possible?

THE ODIN BROTHERHOOD: If the will is sufficiently strong—if its power is sufficiently awesome—any thing that can be imagined can be realized.

AUTHOR: If what you declare is true, why are not miracles more common?

THE ODIN BROTHERHOOD: Because most mortals can wish—only extraordinary mortals can will.

The Fair Goddess Idun and Her Enchanted Fruit

AUTHOR: When you first mentioned Bragi, you noted that he had a wife named Idun.

THE ODIN BROTHERHOOD: Yes. The god of the eloquent words is married to Idun, the shapely goddess of youth.

AUTHOR: Tell me about this Idun.

THE ODIN BROTHERHOOD: Soft and flawless as freshly fallen snow, Idun is the patroness of all that is new and fresh.

AUTHOR: Idun sounds beautiful.

THE ODIN BROTHERHOOD: Yes. And Idun is also one of the most important of the Asgardian goddesses, for she is the keeper of the magic food.

AUTHOR: The magic food?

THE ODIN BROTHERHOOD: The peaches of youth.

AUTHOR: What are the peaches of youth?

THE ODIN BROTHERHOOD: Also called ambrosia, soma, or the apples of life, the peaches of youth are enchanted fruits that grow on a unique tree native to Asgard.

AUTHOR: And why are the fruits special?

THE ODIN BROTHERHOOD: Ripened by the childlike purity of Idun's thoughts, the peaches of youth have the power to reverse the ravages of time.

AUTHOR: You mean, he who eats the peaches becomes young again?

THE ODIN BROTHERHOOD: Yes. Like the elixir of life of the alchemists, Idun's fruit renews and refreshes the bodies and souls of men and gods.

AUTHOR: Gods? So the gods also suffer the effects of old age?

THE ODIN BROTHERHOOD: Of course. The natural lifetime of a god is vast, but even a god ultimately experiences senescence.

AUTHOR: In some religious traditions, the gods are ageless and atemporal. They exist beyond time, where past and future fuse into an absolute present.

THE ODIN BROTHERHOOD: In our universe, time erodes all forms of being. And the power of time—the violence of time—is especially obvious in Asgard. In that ancient city, all beings age more rapidly.

AUTHOR: So the passage of time is not everywhere the same? Time is not symmetrical throughout nature?

THE ODIN BROTHERHOOD: That is correct. An instant in the reality of the gods is an epoch in the reality of men.

AUTHOR: If that is true, what happens to an ordinary mortal who finds the gate and enters the reality of the gods?

THE ODIN BROTHERHOOD: Without the magic food, the results would be disastrous.

AUTHOR: Can you elaborate?

THE ODIN BROTHERHOOD: After a few moments, an ordinary mortal would be dead. After a few moments more, he would be a putrescent corpse. After one night in Asgard, his body would be a heap of black ashes.

AUTHOR: Clearly, visiting Asgard is a perilous enterprise.

THE ODIN BROTHERHOOD: Without the help of youth, all enterprises are dangerous. That is the reason Idun is important.

Brave Tyr, the Warrior God

AUTHOR: Tell me about another one of your deities.

THE ODIN BROTHERHOOD: Another significant deity is Tyr the One-Handed, the brave god who inspires fear but never feels fear himself.

AUTHOR: And why is Tyr called "the One-Handed."

THE ODIN BROTHERHOOD: Because Tyr is disabled. He was mutilated by violence.

AUTHOR: A god can suffer injury?

THE ODIN BROTHERHOOD: The gods are neither invulnerable nor invincible.

AUTHOR: So your gods know the thrill of danger?

THE ODIN BROTHERHOOD: That is correct.

AUTHOR: Regarding Tyr, how was he injured?

THE ODIN BROTHERHOOD: The god sacrificed his hand to neutralize a threat and save Asgard. As the bravest of the gods, Tyr is also the most generous.

AUTHOR: Are bravery and generosity always found together?

THE ODIN BROTHERHOOD: Of course. Selfishness is the spawn of cowardice.

AUTHOR: Regarding bravery, how would you define this virtue?

THE ODIN BROTHERHOOD: There are many forms of bravery, but the supreme form of courage is the one against the all.

AUTHOR: And the supreme form of cowardice?

THE ODIN BROTHERHOOD: The all against the one.

AUTHOR: As a god of bravery, is Tyr a god of battle?

THE ODIN BROTHERHOOD: Yes. Tyr delights in the fury of combat, and he is the patron of all true warriors.

AUTHOR: True warriors?

THE ODIN BROTHERHOOD: Combatants who remember the three prohibitions.

AUTHOR: What are the three prohibitions?

THE ODIN BROTHERHOOD: This is the first: in combat, never fight an unworthy foe.

AUTHOR: An unworthy foe?

THE ODIN BROTHERHOOD: One who is weaker.

AUTHOR: And what is the second prohibition?

THE ODIN BROTHERHOOD: In combat, never kill at a distance.

AUTHOR: In modern war, virtually all killing occurs at a distance.

THE ODIN BROTHERHOOD: That is the reason modern war is criminal—it has made killing and dying anonymous.

AUTHOR: And what is the third prohibition?

THE ODIN BROTHERHOOD: In combat, never retreat before the enemy.

AUTHOR: A true warrior will retreat under no circumstances whatever?

THE ODIN BROTHERHOOD: When a true warrior steps back, it is only to leap forward. That is the teaching of Tyr.

The God Njord, Magic, and the Vanir Gods

AUTHOR: Tell me about another one of your gods.

THE ODIN BROTHERHOOD: Another interesting deity is Njord, the god who is fond of the salt, the sea, and the wind. Although Njord presently lives in Asgard with his wife, he is a Vanir by birth.

AUTHOR: Who are the Vanir?

THE ODIN BROTHERHOOD: Known to fable as the "resplendent ones," the Vanir are beautiful gods and goddesses renowned for the power of their magic.

AUTHOR: And what is magic?

THE ODIN BROTHERHOOD: Magic is a species of knowledge.

AUTHOR: And how does magic differ from other forms of knowledge?

THE ODIN BROTHERHOOD: Magic is the technology of gods. According to some legends, it was invented in Vanir-World.

AUTHOR: Vanir-World?

THE ODIN BROTHERHOOD: The home of the Vanir and the original home of Njord. It is a place of color, music, and scent.

AUTHOR: Where is Vanir-World?

THE ODIN BROTHERHOOD: In the reality of the gods, the birthplace of Njord is located somewhere to the east of Asgard.

AUTHOR: And is there a portal that leads to Vanir-World on Earth?

THE ODIN BROTHERHOOD: Yes. The same aperture that leads to Asgard leads to Vanir-World.

AUTHOR: Since they exist in the same reality, do the Vanir gods commonly visit the gods of Asgard?

THE ODIN BROTHERHOOD: Yes. But that was not always the case.

AUTHOR: Why?

THE ODIN BROTHERHOOD: In ancient times—long before our ancestors walked the Earth—the gods of Vanir-

World and the gods of Asgard waged a war which involved a sorceress named "The-Power-of-Gold."

AUTHOR: And that war is now ended?

THE ODIN BROTHERHOOD: Yes. The war was long and bitter, but at length the universe experienced an armistice of the gods.

AUTHOR: And what maintains the peace?

THE ODIN BROTHERHOOD: The deities of Vanir-World sent two of their number to live in Asgard, and the deities of Asgard sent two of their number to live in Vanir-World.

AUTHOR: So the two sides exchanged hostages?

THE ODIN BROTHERHOOD: That is correct. And in this exchange, Njord and his son went to Asgard.

AUTHOR: And how long will Njord remain in Asgard?

THE ODIN BROTHERHOOD: According to the legends, Njord will stay with the Asgardians until the destruction of this universe.

The God Frey and the Elves

AUTHOR: You mentioned Njord's son also went to Asgard. Who is this son?

THE ODIN BROTHERHOOD: He is called Frey, and he is the king of the elves.

AUTHOR: And who are the elves?

THE ODIN BROTHERHOOD: Known in the legends as "The-People-Who-Walk-In-The-Sky," Frey's subjects are a race of virgins.

AUTHOR: A race of virgins?

THE ODIN BROTHERHOOD: Most elves are chaste, for elves cannot survive procreation.

AUTHOR: An unfortunate curse.

THE ODIN BROTHERHOOD: Yes. For an elf, love-play can lead to death.

AUTHOR: In terms of appearance, do the elves resemble gods?

THE ODIN BROTHERHOOD: Frey's subjects are beautiful entities with statuesque bodies and eyes the color of melted copper.

AUTHOR: And where do these elves live?

THE ODIN BROTHERHOOD: In Elf-world, a place of beauty and fantasy filled with wonderful things.

AUTHOR: Wonderful things?

THE ODIN BROTHERHOOD: Enchanted things—such as mountains of crystal and forests of giant mushrooms.

AUTHOR: And where is this Elf-World located?

THE ODIN BROTHERHOOD: Frey's realm is where every river begins.

AUTHOR: Explain.

THE ODIN BROTHERHOOD: Rain is where every river begins, so Elf-World is somewhere in the architecture of the clouds.

The Goddess Freyja, the Lovely Patroness of Birth

AUTHOR: Tell me about another one of your deities.

THE ODIN BROTHERHOOD: Another significant goddess is Freyja. A Vanir by birth, Freyja has freely joined her father (Njord) and her brother (Frey) in Asgard.

AUTHOR: Describe Freyja.

THE ODIN BROTHERHOOD: Freyja is all that is perfect and feminine. The divine prototype of loveliness—radiating happiness and grace—Freyja epitomizes the woman who inspires our dreams, shapes our hopes, and steals our desires.

AUTHOR: Freyja sounds enchanting.

THE ODIN BROTHERHOOD: Yes. And as she walks through our reality, the power of her beauty causes flowers to blossom and fruits to ripen.

AUTHOR: And what attracts Freyja to our world?

THE ODIN BROTHERHOOD: Lovely Freyja is a fertility goddess. The patroness of all who conceive in pleasure and deliver in pain, Freyja loves to visit young women who are pregnant with new life.

AUTHOR: Does the goddess visit such women often?

THE ODIN BROTHERHOOD: Yes. And Freyja especially enjoys the company of women who are actually in the process of giving birth.

AUTHOR: Childbirth is a sacred time. Uniquely sublime, birth has been called the most common violence experienced by humans.

THE ODIN BROTHERHOOD: Yes. Freyja loves to watch the light enter a newborn baby's eyes, and she also loves to witness the moment when a child first receives its name.

AUTHOR: Why is the naming important?

THE ODIN BROTHERHOOD: According to the legends, a child does not exist until it has a name.

AUTHOR: Do Odinists have a special naming ceremony?

THE ODIN BROTHERHOOD: We do.

AUTHOR: Could you describe it for me?

THE ODIN BROTHERHOOD: First, the mother (or the midwife) washes the newborn infant in sky water. Sky water is the rain that falls from the heavens.

AUTHOR: You referred to a mother or a midwife. May a man perform the naming rite?

THE ODIN BROTHERHOOD: No. What is new and fresh is the domain of women.

AUTHOR: I understand. Please continue.

THE ODIN BROTHERHOOD: Holding the child in her arms, the mother (midwife) declares:

*My son (daughter), faith is a poison that paralyzes the mind.
In all the days of your life, seek knowledge!*

Then, still holding the child, the mother (midwife) speaks these words:

My son (daughter), inactivity is the mother of cowardice, parasitism, and sterility. In all the days of your life, overcome and achieve!

And finally, the mother (midwife) lifts the infant to the sky and declares:

My son (daughter), your name is _____. In honor of Freyja, live well and die bravely.

AUTHOR: Beautiful words.

THE ODIN BROTHERHOOD: Yes. And they are in honor of the most beautiful of all females.

The God Balder and the Adventure of Death

AUTHOR: In terms of beauty, is there a male equivalent of Freyja?

THE ODIN BROTHERHOOD: While he lived, the youthfully handsome Balder was the most desirable god in the eyes of women.

AUTHOR: While he lived? Is Balder dead?

THE ODIN BROTHERHOOD: Yes. Balder, the son of Odin and the husband of Nanna, was the first Asgardian to experience the odyssey called death.

AUTHOR: But how can a god die?

THE ODIN BROTHERHOOD: All gods die. Read, for example, the histories of the dismembered Osiris, the emasculated Attis, and the crucified Christ.

AUTHOR: Your reference to Christ reminds me of the legend—told during medieval times—that Jesus and the goat-god Pan perished on the same day.

THE ODIN BROTHERHOOD: Odinists know and believe that tradition.

AUTHOR: And if gods die, that means all other creatures ultimately die as well?

THE ODIN BROTHERHOOD: Yes. All beings—gods and titans, elves and dwarfs, men and animals—all face certain death and decomposition.

AUTHOR: And how did Balder himself die?

THE ODIN BROTHERHOOD: Invulnerable to fire and water and steel, Balder was killed by a mistletoe projectile that pierced his heart.

AUTHOR: Who hurled the projectile?

THE ODIN BROTHERHOOD: The blind god named Hod. The action was an accident, but Hod nevertheless paid for the mistake with his own life.

AUTHOR: The two deaths sound tragic.

THE ODIN BROTHERHOOD: In a sense. Remember, however, that death is also a benefactress.

AUTHOR: In what way?

THE ODIN BROTHERHOOD: It is necessary. Without death, life would eventually become a spiral of infinite boredom.

AUTHOR: So death gives value to life?

THE ODIN BROTHERHOOD: That is correct. Life is intense because it is limited.

AUTHOR: From the Odinist perspective, what is death?

THE ODIN BROTHERHOOD: In poetic terms, death itself is personified as beautiful females who exist in an endless variety of exquisite forms. These females are called the valkyries.

AUTHOR: And these valkyries extinguish life?

THE ODIN BROTHERHOOD: Yes. The gentle hands of the valkyries softly and voluptuously do the work of killing.

AUTHOR: In the legends, do the valkyries speak to their victims?

THE ODIN BROTHERHOOD: With their fresh, full, and adorable lips, the "daughters of ruin" utter one word in the primordial tongue.

AUTHOR: And what is the one word the valkyries utter?

THE ODIN BROTHERHOOD: No living entity knows "The-Word-That-Excites-Terror," for those who hear it are already embraced by death.

AUTHOR: But Balder now knows the word?

THE ODIN BROTHERHOOD: That is correct.

AUTHOR: You have described death in poetic terms. What is death in concrete terms?

THE ODIN BROTHERHOOD: According to the legends of Balder, death occurs when the entire soul leaves the tabernacle that is the body.

AUTHOR: And does the soul survive death?

THE ODIN BROTHERHOOD: Death is not annihilation, so the soul will endure.

AUTHOR: In Odinist terms, what is a soul?

THE ODIN BROTHERHOOD: A soul is a transfigured life-form. Utterly pure, it has the color and texture of light.

AUTHOR: And what is the shape of the soul?

THE ODIN BROTHERHOOD: The soul is an approximate replica of the body before the body was touched by the cause of death.

AUTHOR: After the soul has exited the body, what does it experience?

THE ODIN BROTHERHOOD: As Balder discovered, the soul is translated to one of three possible Other-Worlds on the opposite shore of existence.

AUTHOR: Describe these "Other-Worlds."

THE ODIN BROTHERHOOD: They are realms governed by dream-logic.

AUTHOR: Dream-logic?

THE ODIN BROTHERHOOD: The state in which all things are possible and nothing is true.

AUTHOR: Are these Other-Worlds heavens—paradises that are quiet, carefree, and vast? Or are they hells—prisons that are vicious, stygian, and stifling?

THE ODIN BROTHERHOOD: They are neither.

AUTHOR: Then what are they?

THE ODIN BROTHERHOOD: All worlds are what we make them.

AUTHOR: You mentioned there are three Other-Worlds. What are their names?

THE ODIN BROTHERHOOD: The first is called White-Kingdom or Valhalla. Heroes who die violent deaths go there.

AUTHOR: Is a violent death absolutely necessary to enter White-Kingdom?

THE ODIN BROTHERHOOD: Yes. Unless a soul exits through a gaping wound, it cannot enter White-Kingdom.

AUTHOR: In an ancient text called *The Ynglinga Saga*, Snorri Sturluson declares that some dying heroes mark their bodies with the points of spears. Is that custom still followed?

THE ODIN BROTHERHOOD: If there is blood at death—no matter how small the offering—the soul finds Valhalla.

A man who knows that secret holds the key to White-Kingdom.

AUTHOR: And what is the second Other-World?

THE ODIN BROTHERHOOD: The second Other-World is called Gray-Kingdom. People who die straw deaths go there.

AUTHOR: Straw deaths?

THE ODIN BROTHERHOOD: People who die in bed from old age or sickness. Their souls exit through the nose/mouth.

AUTHOR: And Gray-Kingdom is open only to the souls of such people?

THE ODIN BROTHERHOOD: That is correct.

AUTHOR: And what is the third Other-World?

THE ODIN BROTHERHOOD: The third Other-World is called Black-Kingdom.

AUTHOR: And who goes there?

THE ODIN BROTHERHOOD: Men and women who are assassinated by sorcery. Their souls exit through the eyes.

AUTHOR: And what is sorcery?

THE ODIN BROTHERHOOD: A species of illicit magic.

AUTHOR: Can you be more exact?

THE ODIN BROTHERHOOD: Sorcery is killing with words.

AUTHOR: And who uses sorcery?

THE ODIN BROTHERHOOD: Ghouls, wizards, and all who thrive on malice.

The Goddess Nanna and the Odinist Death Rite

AUTHOR: Earlier, you mentioned that all gods will ultimately die. After Balder and Hod, who was the next deity to meet the challenge of death?

THE ODIN BROTHERHOOD: The goddess named Nanna, the beloved wife of Balder, was the next Asgardian to die.

AUTHOR: How did Nanna meet her end?

THE ODIN BROTHERHOOD: When Nanna saw her husband on the funeral pyre, she died of grief. Ever since that tragic event, Nanna has been considered the patroness of the Odinist death ritual.

AUTHOR: Tell me about your death ritual.

THE ODIN BROTHERHOOD: When an Odinist dies, one who shares his secret knowledge will perform a special ceremony. This ceremony is called "The-Rite-of-Nanna."

AUTHOR: Please describe it to me.

THE ODIN BROTHERHOOD: The celebrant (the person

performing the rite) must declare in the presence of the corpse the ancient words:

The warrior named _____ is dead. Behold the hero! He (she) died the death of a master—not a servant!

Then, facing the sun, the celebrant, makes this declaration:

The warrior named_____is dead. Behold the hero! Even as the wild flowers return in the spring, so shall he (she) return!

AUTHOR: And is the body cremated or inhumed?

THE ODIN BROTHERHOOD: In ancient times, the body was incinerated. In the current age, however, the body of the dead Odinist must be placed in a standing position in a mound of earth.

AUTHOR: Why are the remains buried upright? It is interesting that Michel de Notredame—the fabled Nostradamus—was entombed in a vertical position.

THE ODIN BROTHERHOOD: Upright is the posture of a warrior. When a man stands erect, he is poised for action.

AUTHOR: After the warrior is inhumed, is the ceremony finished?

THE ODIN BROTHERHOOD: No. The celebrant will conclude the ceremony by burying three objects in the mound with the remains.

AUTHOR: What are the objects?

THE ODIN BROTHERHOOD: One is an acorn. This will cause a mighty oak to mark the site of the grave.

AUTHOR: And the second object?

THE ODIN BROTHERHOOD: A tablet made from the purest lead. If the time is winter, the tablet will be "reddened" with the blood of a living animal and will bear a personal communication to the deceased.

AUTHOR: And the third object?

THE ODIN BROTHERHOOD: The celebrant must insert a broken monolith of solid gold into the mound. This monolith always bears an inscription.

AUTHOR: What does the inscription declare?

THE ODIN BROTHERHOOD: The following words are engraved in the gold:

The warrior named _____ is dead. Behold the hero! He (she) lives in a new form!

AUTHOR: Why is the monolith broken?

THE ODIN BROTHERHOOD: For the deceased to enjoy the grave goods in the next world, the goods must first be "killed." Breaking (or burning) is a way of killing an object.

AUTHOR: How large is the monolith?

THE ODIN BROTHERHOOD: Typically, the monolith is the size of a man's fist. Sometimes, however, it is much larger.

AUTHOR: What is the largest of which you have knowledge?

THE ODIN BROTHERHOOD: According to our legends, the three founders of the Odin Brotherhood ("Mocking-Defiance," "The-Power-of-Innocence," and "Desire-to-Rebel") were buried together in a special mound called "The-Mountain-of-Promise." Tradition states that each of the three monoliths placed with their bodies was the size of a living man.

The Legend of "The-Mountain-of-Promise"

AUTHOR: Such a quantity of gold–such an ancient hoard— must represent an invaluable treasure. Do you know the location of "The-Mountain-of-Promise"?

THE ODIN BROTHERHOOD: No one is certain. According to the legends, however, there are certain clues that will help the seeker.

AUTHOR: What are these clues?

THE ODIN BROTHERHOOD: First, the seeker must find the place where the wood becomes flesh.

AUTHOR: Since an Odinist legend states the first man and woman were cut from trees, this first clue apparently refers to the site where the first humans were made.

THE ODIN BROTHERHOOD: That would seem to be the case.

AUTHOR: And where is that site?

THE ODIN BROTHERHOOD: No one is certain, but the legends say it is located by a body of water—perhaps the Black Sea.

AUTHOR: And the second clue?

THE ODIN BROTHERHOOD: Next, the seeker must walk until he finds the mud that is made by fire rather than by water.

AUTHOR: When soil is frozen, one needs fire—not water—to make mud. So the second clue refers to a place where permafrost exists?

THE ODIN BROTHERHOOD: That would seem to be the case. That is the reason some believe the second clue refers to the top of a mountain.

AUTHOR: And what is the next clue?

THE ODIN BROTHERHOOD: The seeker must walk toward the setting sun until he discovers the painted cave that is located between the sound that never ceases and the cliff shaped like a woman.

AUTHOR: And what do those clues mean?

THE ODIN BROTHERHOOD: No one is certain, but in the ancient poetry we know a cascade is sometimes called "The-Sound-That-Never-Ceases."

AUTHOR: And what is the next clue?

THE ODIN BROTHERHOOD: The seeker must enter the cave and search until he finds the rock dwarf that dared to face the sun.

AUTHOR: Earlier, you mentioned that the power of the sun turned rock dwarfs into stone, so this last clue apparently refers to a stone statue of some sort.

THE ODIN BROTHERHOOD: That would seem to be the case.

AUTHOR: And what is the next clue?

THE ODIN BROTHERHOOD: With the dwarf at his right hand, the seeker must walk until he locates "The-Crypt-of-Secrets." "The-Crypt-of-Secrets" contains "The-Scroll-of-Knowledge" that will lead to "The-Mountain-of-Promise."

AUTHOR: And how will the seeker recognize "The-Crypt-of-Secrets"?

THE ODIN BROTHERHOOD: The crypt is located between the rock that bleeds and the river that laughs.

AUTHOR: These last clues seem unintelligible.

THE ODIN BROTHERHOOD: Odinism thrives on mystery. Mystery, as all sages understand, is fuel for thought.

AUTHOR: But how could anyone possibly solve the riddle and find "The-Mountain-of-Promise"?

THE ODIN BROTHERHOOD: In spite of the seemingly impenetrable nature of the mystery, we know the treasure will one day be discovered.

AUTHOR: And how can you be so certain?

THE ODIN BROTHERHOOD: Before she died, Nanna uttered this prophecy:

*When the world is pregnant with lies, a secret long hidden will
be revealed.*

AUTHOR: And you believe this prophecy refers to "The-
Mountain-of-Promise"?

THE ODIN BROTHERHOOD: Some day the three
monoliths will be unearthed, and the discovery will confirm
the truth of our traditions.

AUTHOR: You are certain of this?

THE ODIN BROTHERHOOD: It is the decree of destiny.

Destiny, Ragnarok, and the Mysteries of the Future

AUTHOR: Destiny? In Odinist terms, what is destiny?

THE ODIN BROTHERHOOD: The Fates, the Moirai,
the Parcae, the Norns—destiny is an enigma with many
names.

AUTHOR: But what is it?

THE ODIN BROTHERHOOD: Destiny is a force implicit
in nature. Personified by three mysterious females called
Urd ("That-Which-Has-Become"), Verdandi ("That-Which-
Is-Still-Becoming"), and Skuld ("That-Which-Is-Owed"),
destiny is the indifferent, irrational, and irrevocable power
that weaves and shapes all realities.

AUTHOR: Even the reality of the gods?

THE ODIN BROTHERHOOD: Even the gods are not above the blameless inevitability that wise men call destiny.

AUTHOR: And how do you know that?

THE ODIN BROTHERHOOD: Because the past, the present, and the future occur without their consent.

AUTHOR: So in all realities, no one is truly free?

THE ODIN BROTHERHOOD: All rational beings— from the lowest man to the highest god—possess the liberty that is important.

AUTHOR: And what liberty is that?

THE ODIN BROTHERHOOD: We cannot choose the joys or the terrors we must face, but we can choose to face them calmly. That is our freedom.

AUTHOR: And what terror must the gods confront?

THE ODIN BROTHERHOOD: Merciless destiny has decreed that the race of lords must experience Ragnarok.

AUTHOR: Ragnarok?

THE ODIN BROTHERHOOD: The end of the universe. The time of devastation and havoc when the gods will see death in a thousand forms.

AUTHOR: When will this Ragnarok occur?

THE ODIN BROTHERHOOD: No one is certain, but this universe is ripe for destruction when man sees the spores of decadence spreading throughout all realities.

AUTHOR: Spores of decadence?

THE ODIN BROTHERHOOD: Corrosive poisons that destroy all integrity.

AUTHOR: And what will happen when these poisons spread?

THE ODIN BROTHERHOOD: Mankind will become a bloody and suppurating sore, rotten to the bone.

AUTHOR: Can you be more specific?

THE ODIN BROTHERHOOD: First, man will become weak, and his greatness will flee.

AUTHOR: And second?

THE ODIN BROTHERHOOD: People will go against nature, and women will become men and men will become children.

AUTHOR: And is there a third?

THE ODIN BROTHERHOOD: The shameless will become worse, and traditional perversions will no longer gratify. On this last point, listen to what the ancient prophecies declare:

> *daughters and sons*
> *incestuously mix;*
> *man is a plaything*
> *of mighty whoredoms...*
> *before the World ends.*

AUTHOR: Based on what you have said, the spores of decadence are already with us.

THE ODIN BROTHERHOOD: Yes. They spread like polyps in unwholesome flesh, but fortunately the infestation is not yet ubiquitous.

AUTHOR: And is that significant?

THE ODIN BROTHERHOOD: Indeed. As long as men and women live in the legion of honor, Ragnarok will not occur.

AUTHOR: Are you suggesting that the existence of Odinists is postponing the end of the world?

THE ODIN BROTHERHOOD: When the last hero dies, the process of inexorable destruction will begin.

AUTHOR: Regarding the destruction, what will happen?

THE ODIN BROTHERHOOD: First there will be three years without a summer. The legends call this period "The-Season-of-Untimely-Doom." Next, the sun and the moon will enter "The-Tomb-of-Worlds." That is to say, the sun and the moon will perish.

AUTHOR: And then what will happen?

THE ODIN BROTHERHOOD: The ancient barriers that separate all realities will groan and split, all fetters will burst, and the traditional enemies of the gods will run, walk, and crawl from their sanctuaries, lairs, and prisons to make war on the forces of Asgard.

AUTHOR: By enemies, you are referring to the frost giants and the fire giants?

THE ODIN BROTHERHOOD: Yes. And these titans will be assisted by an infamous army of apocalyptic monsters.

AUTHOR: Apocalyptic monsters?

THE ODIN BROTHERHOOD: Trolls with an insatiable appetite for destruction. Ancient adversaries of the race of lords, the most lethal are called "The-Wolf-That-Feeds-On-Gods," "The-World-Serpent," and the death-hound named "Garm."

AUTHOR: These creatures sound inconceivably powerful.

THE ODIN BROTHERHOOD: Yes. And to increase their fury is to increase their strength.

AUTHOR: These creatures also sound inconceivably evil.

THE ODIN BROTHERHOOD: The trolls are innocent of crime.

AUTHOR: They are not wicked in any way?

THE ODIN BROTHERHOOD: The trolls are dangerous not because of their sins, but because of their power.

AUTHOR: But if the trolls are not wicked, who is?

THE ODIN BROTHERHOOD: In an absolute sense, no one is wicked. Everything is perspective.

AUTHOR: Perspective? Explain.

THE ODIN BROTHERHOOD: Consider a dove. To a man, that bird is an exquisite, benevolent, and inoffensive creature. But to a worm that is mangled and devoured by that selfsame bird, the dove is a depraved monster of unparalleled cruelty.

AUTHOR: But if evil does not exist, are all things permitted?

THE ODIN BROTHERHOOD: Not at all. There is no evil, but there is dishonor.

AUTHOR: And what is dishonor?

THE ODIN BROTHERHOOD: A form of impurity, dishonor is anything that changes our nature and steals from us our souls.

AUTHOR: Well, let us return to the subject of Ragnarok.

THE ODIN BROTHERHOOD: Yes. We were discussing omnicide on a cosmic level.

AUTHOR: In the final days, how will the gods respond to the attack by the titans and the trolls?

THE ODIN BROTHERHOOD: Heimdall, the vigilant warder of Asgard, will stand forth and sound a warning that will be heard throughout all realities. As soon as Odin perceives the warning, he will hasten to "The-Well-of-Wisdom" to consult the one called Mimir.

AUTHOR: And who is Mimir?

THE ODIN BROTHERHOOD: Dark, proud, and introspective, Mimir is the teacher of those who know.

AUTHOR: And what makes Mimir so wise?

THE ODIN BROTHERHOOD: More than any other

entity, Mimir knows the secrets of the past, the intricacies of the present, and the mysteries of the future.

AUTHOR: And what words will be exchanged at "The-Well-of-Wisdom"?

THE ODIN BROTHERHOOD: According to the prophecies, Odin will declare:

> *O Mimir, a vast horde is arrayed against the empire of the gods. Is victory possible for Asgard?*

And Mimir will reply:

> *O Odin, in the battle that will decide the future, the gods face certain defeat. Destiny has targeted Asgard for annihilation.*

AUTHOR: And how will Odin respond to such grim news?

THE ODIN BROTHERHOOD: Austere as platinum, Odin will say:

> *A heroic death is the apex of glory. In spite of the futility of the task, I will lead a bold attack against our enemies.*

AUTHOR: And what will happen next?

THE ODIN BROTHERHOOD: Mimir will speak the last words he will utter in this universe. He will declare:

> *Go with my friendship, brave Odin. And remember, you will find freedom in the final defiance.*

AUTHOR: So, after talking to Mimir, Odin will gather his forces?

THE ODIN BROTHERHOOD: Yes. With an enchanted spear in hand, Odin will muster his warriors.

AUTHOR: Describe Odin's army.

THE ODIN BROTHERHOOD: All-Father will lead two battalions. The first will be composed of gods and goddesses.

AUTHOR: All the deities we have discussed?

THE ODIN BROTHERHOOD: All those deities plus the gods named Vidar ("The-God-Who-Dares-All-And-Says-Nothing"), Vali ("The-God-Who-Avenges"), Ull ("The-Magnificent-Hunter"), Forseti ("The-Warlike-And-Studious-One"), Hermod ("The-Intrepid-One"), Hoenir, ("The-Hostage-God-Who-Returns"), Vili ("The-Mysterious-One"), and Ve ("The-Venerable-One"), together with the goddesses named Gefjun ("The-Virgin-Combatant"), Eir ("The-Goddess-Who-Heals"), Fulla ("The-Protector-of-Secrets"), Saga ("The-Goddess-Who-Sees-All-Things"), Lofn ("The-Goddess-Whose-Heart-Is-Mild"), Jord ("The-Mother-of-Strength"), Hlin ("The-Protector-of-Heroes"), Sjofn ("The-Friend-of-Lovers"), Var ("The-Goddess-Who-Desires-All-Wisdom"), Snotra ("The-Prudent-One"), Syn ("She-Whose-Name-Means-Denial"), Ran ("The-Friend-of-All-Who-Perish-at-Sea"), Vor ("She-Whose-Name-Means-Awareness"), and Gna ("The-Goddess-Who-Soars-on-Magic").

AUTHOR: Will Loki stand with the Asgardians in the final battle?

THE ODIN BROTHERHOOD: Loki is a frost giant by

birth. In the war that terminates this universe, he will rejoin his natural brothers.

AUTHOR: You said Odin will lead a second battalion. Who will make up the second battalion?

THE ODIN BROTHERHOOD: Brave souls from fabled Valhalla, the Other-World on the opposite shore of existence.

AUTHOR: So Odin will command a battalion of the dead?

THE ODIN BROTHERHOOD: Yes. Those who died of violence will have the courage to face the violence that is Ragnarok.

AUTHOR: And what about those who died of sickness, old age, or sorcery?

THE ODIN BROTHERHOOD: In the final days, they will be incapacitated by the worm of fear.

AUTHOR: When the battle called Ragnarok begins, who will strike the first blow?

THE ODIN BROTHERHOOD: Odin will hurl his spear at the sky, and it will fall back crimson with blood.

AUTHOR: And then what will happen?

THE ODIN BROTHERHOOD: At the vanguard of his Asgardian host, Odin will grapple with "The-Wolf-That-Feeds-On-Gods."

AUTHOR: And will Odin defeat the beast?

THE ODIN BROTHERHOOD: The creature will kill and

devour "All-Father," but Odin will be avenged by his son, Vidar the Silent.

AUTHOR: And how will Vidar avenge his father?

THE ODIN BROTHERHOOD: Mute until this time, Vidar will approach the wolf and utter these words:

> *You have shown you have the courage to kill. Do you have the courage to die?*

Then, using steel against bone, Vidar will cut the wolf's breath from his body.

AUTHOR: After Odin has died and Vidar has avenged him, how will the war progress?

THE ODIN BROTHERHOOD: Thor, the slayer of trolls, will fight "The-World-Serpent."

AUTHOR: Describe Thor's battle.

THE ODIN BROTHERHOOD: The struggle will be titanic. The Earth itself will convulse and shake, and lightning will play about the combatants.

AUTHOR: And how will this combat end?

THE ODIN BROTHERHOOD: Knee deep in blood and gore, the mighty Thor will crush the serpent's body and dismember its soul.

AUTHOR: So Thor will be victorious over the reptilian horror?

THE ODIN BROTHERHOOD: Yes. But after taking nine steps, Thor himself will die of his adversary's venom.

AUTHOR: And what will happen next?

THE ODIN BROTHERHOOD: Tyr will die killing the death hound named Garm, Heimdall and Loki will find mutual annihilation in a plain strewn with bones, Freyja will slay several dragons before she herself is killed, Idun will be soiled and raped and murdered, and countless warriors will disappear in an environment thick with capricious death.

AUTHOR: The combat sounds ferocious.

THE ODIN BROTHERHOOD: The universe will become a mass grave for gods and men, titans and trolls.

AUTHOR: And when will it become clear that the gods and their allies will suffer defeat?

THE ODIN BROTHERHOOD: When the brave god named Frey falls in battle.

AUTHOR: And who will vanquish this god?

THE ODIN BROTHERHOOD: After an effusion of blood, Frey will be killed by a mighty fire giant named Surt.

AUTHOR: And your prophecies are certain on this point? Surt will defeat Frey?

THE ODIN BROTHERHOOD: The prophecies are exact. These are the ancient words:

> *On his dagger, Surt will one day hold aloft the bleeding head of Frey.*

AUTHOR: And why will this one deity's death be a turning point?

THE ODIN BROTHERHOOD: Because once Frey is destroyed, Surt will fulfill his ultimate destiny.

AUTHOR: And what is the ultimate destiny of Surt?

THE ODIN BROTHERHOOD: Surt will have the honor of laying waste to the universe.

AUTHOR: Destroying the universe is an honor?

THE ODIN BROTHERHOOD: Of course. Destruction is a form of hygiene. Natural and necessary, destruction makes room for new worlds.

AUTHOR: So destruction—like death—is a benefactress?

THE ODIN BROTHERHOOD: That is correct.

AUTHOR: And Surt will be the tool of this benefactress?

THE ODIN BROTHERHOOD: Yes. And Surt understands his destiny. Even now, he toys with his weapon and waits for the time ordained by fate.

AUTHOR: And how will Surt destroy the universe?

THE ODIN BROTHERHOOD: According to our legends, the end of this universe will recall its beginning.

AUTHOR: Explain.

THE ODIN BROTHERHOOD: In a conflagration this universe was born, and in a storm of fire—an orgy of purification— this universe will die.

AUTHOR: And Surt will unleash this storm of fire?

THE ODIN BROTHERHOOD: Yes. He will send a wall of liquid flame across all realities.

AUTHOR: Undoubtedly, that will be an awesome sight.

THE ODIN BROTHERHOOD: Yes, terrible to behold, the gods will see obliteration in a flash of wild beauty.

AUTHOR: And when will this process of destruction stop?

THE ODIN BROTHERHOOD: The destruction will stop when there is nothing left to violate.

AUTHOR: After Surt has fulfilled his destiny, what will happen next?

THE ODIN BROTHERHOOD: Few can see beyond "The-Great-Purification."

AUTHOR: But what do your prophecies declare?

THE ODIN BROTHERHOOD: According to the legends, the pulverized remains of this universe will give birth to a new universe.

AUTHOR: So a new order will emerge from disorder?

THE ODIN BROTHERHOOD: That is correct.

AUTHOR: Describe that new universe.

THE ODIN BROTHERHOOD: It will have the purity that exists before exhaustion and decay.

AUTHOR: And will there be gods after "The-Great-Purification"?

THE ODIN BROTHERHOOD: Balder and Hod will return from the dead, and they will lead a new race of lords.

AUTHOR: And will there be men after "The-Great-Purification"?

THE ODIN BROTHERHOOD: According to the legends, one man and one woman will escape the holocaust of Surt by taking refuge in "The-World-Tree-of-Knowledge." They will become the parents of the new humanity.

AUTHOR: And do you know the names of the man and the woman?

THE ODIN BROTHERHOOD: They will be called "Life" and "Desire-for-Life."

AUTHOR: And they will be humanity's hope for the future?

THE ODIN BROTHERHOOD: That is their destiny.

AUTHOR: I have one last inquiry. What of Odin, Thor, Frey, and the other gods who will perish? Will they be gone for all eternity?

THE ODIN BROTHERHOOD: Nothing dies forever.

AUTHOR: So the slain gods will return?

THE ODIN BROTHERHOOD: We all return. Life is like a dream that recurs.

AUTHOR: But how is that possible?

THE ODIN BROTHERHOOD: To understand that enigma, you must comprehend "The-Law-of-the-Endless-Circle."

AUTHOR: And what is "The-Law-of-the-Endless-Circle"?

THE ODIN BROTHERHOOD: It is our fundamental mystery.

AUTHOR: Please explain it to me.

THE ODIN BROTHERHOOD: According to this sublime arcanum, time is an endless circle in which all possible destinies are repeated forever.

AUTHOR: And what does that mean in concrete terms?

THE ODIN BROTHERHOOD: All that will happen has happened, and all that has happened will happen again.

AUTHOR: So the gods are characters in a vast drama that is replayed over and over on a cosmic scale?

THE ODIN BROTHERHOOD: That is correct.

AUTHOR: And that is the reason the gods come back?

THE ODIN BROTHERHOOD: The future must be a return to the past. It is "The-Law-of-the-Endless-Circle."

AUTHOR: The concept is an interesting one.

THE ODIN BROTHERHOOD: Yes. And he who understands the mystery will understand the first words that Balder will utter in the new universe.

AUTHOR: What will Balder say?

THE ODIN BROTHERHOOD: Called the supreme paradox, this will be his declaration:

Hail to the gods that are dead! They are the future race of lords!

- Epilogue -

A Statement on the Odin Brotherhood
by Mark L. Mirabello, Ph.D.

I am not an authorized spokesman for the Odin Brotherhood. Because I have revealed secrets, I could be described more accurately as a spy.

My first contact was a silver-haired gentleman in a bookshop in Leith, Scotland. An eastern European, he was holding a peculiar cane adorned with the images of the serpent and the ass. (The serpent and the ass, of course, are the two animals that speak in the Bible.)

We were both examining "occult books," and he noticed I was studying *The Brotherhood of the Rosy Cross* by Arthur Edward Waite. A Christian order dating from the Middle Ages, scholars claim the Brotherhood of the Rosy Cross was "invented" in the seventeenth century.

"The rose symbolizes secrecy," said the stranger, pointing to an engraving in my book. "Since we speak '*sub rosa*' or 'under the rose,' our discussion must remain forever secret."

The man, who whimsically called himself "Lodur's friend" (in honor of the enigmatic god in the *Eddaic Verses*), asked me several details about my life, and with every response he pointed out "meaningful coincidences."

My first and last names, for example, begin with the letter "M." Since "M" is pronounced with the lips closed, it traditionally symbolizes secrecy.

M is also the thirteenth letter of the alphabet, and there are thirteen letters in "Mark Mirabello." Since 13 is unlucky to Christians—thirteen people were present at the "last supper" of the Galilean—the stranger said my name indicated "misfortune" for the Christians.

My father's family originated in the old duchy of Benevento. A medieval center of the Lombards—as well as a place of the Romans, Greeks, and Normans—Benevento was known as a matrix of occultism.

And finally, the stranger pointed out that even my doctoral research at the University of Glasgow was curiously meaningful. My supervisors were Dr. Ian B. Cowan from the University of Glasgow and Dr. David Stevenson from the University of Aberdeen. Curiously, Cowan means "outsider" in occult lore. Stevenson would know that, for he is a leading authority on arcane orders in Scotland.

Several months passed before I saw the stranger again. Our second meeting—another meaningful coincidence—occurred outside the Atlantis Bookshop, an occult emporium near the British Museum.

"Blind loyalty is a virtue in a dog," declared the stranger, when he noticed me studying an obscure essay on faith, "but it is an offense in a human being."

Since I was interested in the stranger's knowledge, we became friends. We began to meet for dinner—usually in Edinburgh or London—and he introduced me to a circle of fascinating individuals.

The dinner assembly, which referred to itself as a conventicle, was by invitation only. Those who "feared" or "hated" authority were excluded. Those who "laughed at" authority, however, were welcome into the group.

We dined only at night—during the time of the new moon. Always, the feast was adjourned before dawn.

It was our custom to eat roast pork. Pork—or more specifically, the flesh of the wild boar—is the customary food of warriors. Since the wild boar feeds on acorns of the oak, the most sacred of trees, it is a consecrated animal. Virile and strong, the wild boar heroically defends its freedom.

Initially, our conventicle discussed orthodox theology. We contrasted, for example, the biblical Satan—who tricked Eve, annoyed Job, and tempted Jesus—with the biblical Jehovah—who drowned planets, cremated cities, and destroyed Egyptian babies.

Ultimately, however, our conversations always focused on arcane lore—especially secret societies. We discussed the Leopard Men of West Africa, the Thuggee cult of India, the Rebels Against the Modern World of Italy, the Thirteen Society of France, the Knights of the Apocalypse of Belgium, and something they called the Odin Brotherhood.

My mysterious friends, who seemed especially versed in the lore of the Odin Brotherhood, described the group as a luminous beacon in a corrupt and squalid world. Consecrated to pagan gods—gods who were older, better, truer—the Brotherhood draws men and women who valued knowledge, freedom, and power.

I was intrigued, for Odinism represented the hero instead of the saint. The mailed fist over the nailed hands!

* * *

Over the years, individuals have asked specific questions about the Odin Brotherhood. I will repeat their questions and my answers here.

Q. Has the Odin Brotherhood existed literally since 1421? According to historians, Lithuania was the last pagan stronghold in Europe. Officially converted in 1386, pagan elements supposedly did not survive beyond the fifteenth century.

A. The Brotherhood's claim is impossible to prove, but it is not extraordinary. The oldest industrial firm in the world— The Fabbrica d'Armi Pietro Beretta S.p.A. in Italy—has existed since 1526 and is now run by an eleventh generation Beretta. If a family business could show a great longevity, why not a secret society/religion?

Gnosticism—a quasi-Christian movement going back to the time of Christ—was once considered extinct by scholars. Of course, that was until the Mandaeans were "rediscovered" in southern Iraq.

The Parsees—followers of Zarathustra who fled to India in the medieval period—once thought their religion had perished in the Iranian homeland. Several centuries after their flight, they discovered that their belief was false.

In history, centuries are nothing. Ma Yu Ching's, a restaurant which opened in China in AD 1153, is still functioning today.

Q. Why do you not provide specific details—names and

places—when you describe the Odin Brotherhood? Even Gerald B. Gardner, who started the Witchcraft revival with *Witchcraft Today*, named his source.

A. Traditional Odin Brotherhood devotees are serious about their anonymity. If asked about the Brotherhood, they will deny they belong and some will deny even the Brotherhood's very existence. They call this "the ruse of the warrior."

On the subject of Gardner, it is an interesting fact that his alleged source was named Dorothy Clutterbuck. Although Clutterbuck's existence has long been denied by academic historians, Doreen Valiente proved through birth and death records that Gardner's source was indeed a real person.

Q. Why is secrecy still necessary today?

A. Odinism thinks strategically rather than tactically. Although ridicule has replaced the stake as the preferred method of persecution, the violence of the "burning times" may some day return. Remember, the future may not be a continuation of the present.

Besides, real heroes are not honored in our decadent time. Our society puts the true hero in a prison or a circus.

Q. Some individuals search for the Brotherhood and never find it. Why is that the case?

A. To see something, you must know how to look. Did ancient Sparta have walls? The barbarians could not see them, but every Greek knew the truth.

The warriors of Sparta were its walls.

People who look for a formal structure—a temple or a post office box—will never find the Brotherhood.

Q. Some witches are solitary practitioners. That is to say, they learn the lore, initiate themselves, and never have contact with a larger group. Are some members of the Brotherhood solitary practitioners?

A. In centuries past, all members of the Brotherhood learned the secrets from older and wiser warriors. Heroes who knew how to rule, fight, hunt, and procreate!

Since I wrote my work, however, solitaries seem to be growing in numbers.

Q. When members of the Odin Brotherhood are solitaries, how do they recognize one another? The initiation lesions cut during "The-Sojourn-of-the-Brave" would not be visible in most circumstances.

A. There are subtle clues that identify a warrior as a member of the Brotherhood. No other Odinists, for example, refer to Idun's magic food as the "peaches of youth."

Q. Your book declares that the gods are real beings who often visit earth. Have the gods made contact with the Brotherhood?

A. That is the belief. Although it seems implausible, I have a letter sent from Hamburg, Germany supposedly from Odin himself. A letter sounds odd—Judaic/Christian culture has conditioned us to think in terms of burning bushes, "clouds of glory," and pillars of fire—but anything is possible.

Ezra Pound, in Canto 113, wrote:

> *The Gods have not returned. They never*
> *left us.*
> *They have not returned.*

Q. Why were you chosen to reveal the secrets?

A. I was not chosen. Remember, I am not an authorized spokesman for the Odin Brotherhood. Because I have revealed secrets, I could be described more accurately as a spy.

Eddaic Sources

There are two important primary sources for Odinism, the *Elder Edda* (*Eddaic Verses*) and the *Younger Edda* (*Prose Edda*).

Several English translations of the *Eddaic Verses* are available. In particular, the reader should consult the following:

Bellows, Henry Adams. *The Poetic Edda: Translated from the Icelandic with an Introduction and Notes*. New York: American Scandinavian Foundation, 1923.

Hollander, Lee M. *The Poetic Edda: Translated with an Introduction and Explanatory Notes*. Austin: University of Texas Press, 1962.

Larrington, Carolyne. *The Poetic Edda: Translated with an Introduction and Notes*. Oxford: Oxford University Press, 1996.

Terry, Patricia. *Poems of the Elder Edda*. Philadelphia: University of Pennsylvania Press, 1990.

For the *Prose Edda*–less reliable than the *Eddaic Verses*–the reader should consult the following translations:

Sturluson, Snorri. *Edda*. Trans. Anthony Faulkes. London: Dent, 1987.

Sturluson, Snorri. *The Prose Edda: Tales from Norse Mythology*. Trans and ed. Jean Young. Berkeley, University of California Press, 1954.

Works on Modern Odinism

Modern Odinism—which is sometimes referred to as Asatru

(an Icelandic term) or Wotanism (a term derived from the German version of Odin's name)—has produced a body of material available in English. Although many works were privately printed, all are available through the internet.

Since Odinists are individualists, some of the books listed are controversial. A few have radical political agendas, and some openly glorify a neo-barbarian way of life. One anonymous text (a book that is distributed gratuitously to seekers) is a copy of another author's work.

Aswynn, Freya. *Northern Mysteries and Magick: Runes, Gods, and Feminine Powers.* St. Paul, Minnesota: Llewellyn Publications, 2002.

The Book of Rites. London: Odinist Fellowship, 2001.

Camp, L. E. *A Handbook of Armanen Runes.* Sandusky, Ohio: Europa Germanic Traditions Ltd, 2001.

Guide to the Runes. Sandusky, Ohio: Odinic Rite-Vinland, 1992.

Gundarsson, Kveldulf, ed. *Our Troth.* Tempe, Arizona: Ring of Troth, 1993.

- - -. *Teutonic Religion: Folk Beliefs and Practices of the Northern Tradition.* St. Paul, Minnesota: Llewellyn, 1992.

- - -. *Teutonic Magic: The Magical and Spiritual Practices of the Germanic Peoples.* St. Paul, Minnesota: Llewellyn, 1990.

Harbard, Sigi. *The New Odinism.* Woodland Hills, California: Asgard Enterprises, 1982.

Interview With a Gothi: Heimgest, DCG-OR, Speaks. Reims

Cedex, France: Institute of Research on Northern Mythology and Identity, 1996.

McNallen, Stephen A. *Rituals of Asatru.* 3 vols. Payson, Arizona: World Tree Publications, 1992.

- - -. *Thunder from the North: The Way of the Teutonic Warrior.* Nevada City, California: Asatru Folk Assemby, 1993.

McVan, Ron. *Creed of Iron–Wotansvolk Wisdom.* Wilmington, North Carolina: 14 Word Press, 1997.

- - -. *Temple of Wotan: Holy Book of the Aryan Tribes.* Wilmington, North Carolina: 14 Word Press, 2000.

Mills, A. Rudd. *The Call of Our Ancient Nordic Religion.* Australia: 1957.

Odinic Mythology. 2 vols. London: Odinic Rite, 2000.

Pennick, Nigel. *Rune Magic: The History and Practice of Ancient Runic Traditions.* London: Thorsons, 1993.

Sheil, Thorr. *Old Norse Mysteries, Deities, and Worship.* New York: Trollwise Pubications, no date.

Slauson, Irv. *The Religion of Odin: A Handbook.* Red Wing, Minnesota: Asatru Free Church Committee, 1978.

Stead, Lewis. *Ravenbok: The Raven Kindred Ritual Book.* Wheaton, Maryland: Asatru Today, 1994.

Storyteller, Ragnar. *Odin's Return.* Payson, Arizona: World Tree Publications, 1995.

Teachings of the Odin Brotherhood. Portland: Thule Publications, no date.

This is Odinism. London: Odinist Committee, 1974.

Thorsson, Edred. *Futhark: A Handbook of Rune Magic.* Boston: Red Wheel/Weiser, 1988.

- - - . *Book of Troth.* St. Paul: Minnesota: Llewellyn Publications, 1989.

Turner, Earl. *The Essentials of Wotanism.* Portland: Thule Publications, 1994.

Von List, Guido. *The Secret of the Runes.* Trans. Stephen Flowers. Rochester, Vermont: Inner Traditions International, 1988.

Wardle, Thorolf. *Rune Lore.* London: Odinic Rite, no date.

Wodanson, Edred. *The World Tree: An Introduction to the Ancient Ancestral Religion of Asatru.* Union Bay, BC, Canada: Wodanesdag Press, 1995.

- - -. *A Way of Wyrd.* Union Bay, BC, Canada: Wodanesdag Press, 1997.

Wulfstan. *Odinism in the Modern World.* London: Odinic Rite, 2002.

Yeowell, John. *Book of Blots: Ceremonies, Rituals and Invocations of the Odinic Rite.* London: Odinic Rite, 1991.

- - -. *Hidden Gods: Period of Dual Faith in England 680-1980.* London: Odinic Rite, 1995.

- - -. *Odinism and Christianity Under the Third Reich.* London: Odinic Rite, 1993.

Reviews of Earlier Editions of
The Odin Brotherhood

1) Dr. Jeffrey Kaplan, in *Radical Religion in America*, **calls** *The Odin Brotherhood*:

> *an interesting account of an Odinist group claiming unbroken succession from the pagan-era Norse.*

2) Ms. Margot Adler, author of *Drawing down the Moon*, **writes in a letter dated April 28, 1993:**

> *I loved your book....Some of the passages seem deeply insightful—even profound—which is rare in this kind of literature.*

3) Mr. Steve McNallen, leader of the Asatru Folk Assembly, author of *Rituals of Asatru*, **editor of** *Runestone*, **writes in a letter dated October 10, 1992:**

> *Thanks you for The Odin Brotherhood. My wife and I read it, entranced.... Concise, powerful turns of phrase are what most impressed us about this document.*

Mr. McNallen, in a review written for *Runestone*:

> *Again, it's not your standard, everyday Odinism—and that's fine with us. There are some lofty ideals here, expressed in words of ringing nobility.*

4) Mr. R. N. Taylor, member of the Asatru Alliance, writes in a review for *Vor Tru*:

Must reading for those into the way of the warrior.

5) Mr. E. Max Hyatt ("Edred Wodanson"), author of *The World Tree* **and founder of Wodan's Kindred in Canada, writes in a letter dated March 1, 1996:**

A very inspirational work indeed.... I (along with everyone present) soon became spellbound by it and I continued to read on. No one spoke or moved during the complete reading and I finished it in a room filled with profound silence (the only way I can describe it). Some of the women folk had tears in their eyes. It was quite a moving experience. The sun was going down and I read the final page in almost total darkness.

I have since given copies of it as gifts to friends and relatives alike–always with a very positive and intense response! I thank you for your very valuable gift of inspiration to Asatru/ Odinsim.

6) In a review for World Tree Publications of the Asatru Alliance:

A fascinating and inspirational account of a dialogue between the author and members of an ancient Odinic Society based in Scotland. You won't find any limp-wristed, New-Age philosophy here, just hard-hitting Asatru realism. Inspirational reading.

7) Mr. Ralph Harrison ("Ingvar"), leader of the Odinist Fellowship, in a review for *Odinism Today*:

...ranges far and wide on Odinist themes, from the errors of

monotheism to Ragnarok; the speaker talks of the Brotherhood's initiation ceremony and, in a particularly fascinating part of the dialogue, he discusses the means of passing from one world to another and the presence of gods walking amongst us in the guise of men and women. Much of what is contained in the dialogue in the way of teaching and theology is very sound and impressively expressed with vigor and imagination and the heroic aspects of Odinist life are emphasized. Indeed, it resembles and could almost serve as an Odinist catechism, if there were to be such a thing.

8) Dr. Graham Harvey, co-author of *Paganism Today* writes:

A book called **The Odin Brotherhood** *has been circulating which claims to be a record of contacts (in Britain and elsewhere) between Dr. Mark Mirabello and a secret society called The Odin Brotherhood. Whilst I have received enigmatic letters claiming to be from members of the group I have been unable to check the veracity of Mirabello's claims.*

9) Mr. Russ Kick, author of *Outposts: A Catalogue of Rare and Disturbing Information,* writes:

Within Odinism there is a secret society known as the Odin Brotherhood. The author came into contact with members of this shadowy group while doing doctoral research at the University of Glasgow in Scotland. He relates the Brotherhood's history and beliefs in this book through an extended dialogue....

Supplement

The following interview of Professor Mark L. Mirabello, the author of *The Odin Brotherhood: A Non-Fiction Account of Contact with a Pagan Secret Society*, was recorded at Shawnee State University. The interview was conducted by Mr. Micah Ross, a researcher who studies secret societies. The interview was prepared for the *Odin Lives* radio program. My name is Michael Neil Reed.

Odin Lives Interview

Q. Professor Mirabello, you describe the Odin Brotherhood as a secret society for "higher men and women" who value "knowledge, freedom, and power."

A. That is correct. The Odin Brotherhood represents strength over weakness, pride over humility, and knowledge over faith. In an era of ugliness, impotence, and death, it glorifies beauty, power, and life.

Q. How would you define a higher man and woman?

A. Higher humans are godlike humans. In contrast to ordinary men and women—people who toil and obey—the higher men and women know how to rule, fight, hunt, and procreate.

Q. From history, can you name a higher man?

A. The famous Spartacus was a hero in life and in death.

Q. What about Samson? Was he a higher man?

A. From a detached perspective, Samson—although brave— was a mass murderer. In the most famous suicide attack before 2001, Samson killed 3,000 children, women, and men when he destroyed himself and a temple of Dagon. The number is from the biblical book of Judges, chapter 16.

Q. As a secret society, is the Odin Brotherhood also a warrior religion?

A. Yes. In an age of iron it is a creed of steel.

Q. Is war not an evil?

A. The modern era—called the Kali Yuga by the Hindus—is a decadent era—a time of treachery, depravity, and sadism—so the modern era has corrupted combat. With modern technology—to cite Baron Evola—we exterminate people like germs and insects. The fabled warrior has been replaced by the annihilationist

Q. But if modern war is corrupt, is a warrior religion necessary?

A. Consider modern life. With all the statute laws and moral codes, the straightjackets and the leg irons, the hangmen and the priests, the Earth is a vast open-air prison. The masses are afraid and compliant. Now—more than ever—we need Promethean figures—heroic warriors.

Q. Ninety per cent of all species that ever existed on Earth are now extinct. Will not the heroic warrior ultimately go the way of the dinosaurs?

A. According to the Odin Brotherhood, when the last human hero dies, the end of this universe will begin. The process—called Ragnarok in the legends—is a time of devastation and havoc.

Q. So the presence of Odinists on Earth is preserving the universe? The universe literally owes its existence to them?

A. The ancient Aztecs taught that by shedding human blood they sustained the universe. Odinists—in contrast—believe that by living heroically they keep the universe alive.

Q. And why is the Brotherhood dedicated to the Norse gods? The gods of the wild north?

A. Diodorus Siculus—a Greek historian who lived in the century of Julius Caesar—said that when truth is corrupted—barbarian people—people untainted by civilization—preserved it unspoilt.

Modern Odinism follows the principles articulated in the ancient poems called the *Eddaic Verses*. In their present form, these *Eddaic Verses* were preserved by the Vikings—brave raiders of the far north—men and women who were as strong and as clear as mountain rivers.

Q. The ancient Vikings were higher men and women?

A. Indeed. They were strong with virility and innocence.

Q. Professor Mirabello, how would you define a secret society?

A. Dr. Alan Axelrod, an expert on such groups, suggests secret societies share three characteristics: they are exclusive, they claim to own special secrets, and they show a strong inclination to favor their own.

Q. Is the Odin Brotherhood the most unusual secret society you have ever encountered?

A. No. I know of another—centered in Italy— that teaches the Roman empire never fell. The group is convinced that the empire survives today—disguised as the Vatican and the mafia.

Q. And why are secret societies important?

A. Because—to cite Hannah Arendt—real power begins where secrecy begins. The current situation in America—in which both presidential candidates belong to the Brotherhood of Death—the so-called Skull and Bones—proves that point.

Q. Until you published your work, the very existence of the Odin Brotherhood was a secret. Why has it been revealed now?

A. The time is right. Astrologically speaking, not only are we at the end of the age of Pisces—the time of the Galilean— but we live in a shameless epoch—a time of lies, holocausts, and abortions—and humanity requires a creed of iron.

On the notion of the rightness of the time, the Tibetans have an interesting concept. They believe that certain hidden revelations—scriptures called the *Terma*—are concealed in caves and secret places. These scriptures are discovered when the human race is ready to receive them.

Q. You claim that Brotherhood was established in 1421?

A. That is the lore.

Q. Can you prove the Brotherhood was established in the 15th century?

A. Persuading skeptics is always a futile task. In the last 2 centuries, over 200 books have been published claiming that Jesus the Nazarene never existed. One work claims that the entire New Testament—and all of the individuals in it— from Mary the Virgin to Paul of Tarsus, from the apostle John to Jesus himself—are fictions fabricated by the Piso family of Rome.

Needless to say, since there are people who claim a billion modern Christians have been duped, there will be people who will never be persuaded that the Brotherhood's claims are true.

Q. And you claim the Brotherhood—although it was persecuted during the "burning times"—has existed in unbroken lineage to the present?

A. As I note in the book, the Brotherhood "bears the teeth marks of Christianity," but it has survived.

Q. Most people believe that all Odinism disappeared during the "burning times."

A. Temples were destroyed—books were burned—Odinists were accused of (to use a biblical phrase) "whoring after strange gods"—but the idea lived. Remember, ideas are difficult to kill. The Romans destroyed Jerusalem TWICE within a century of Jesus's crucifixion, but they failed to kill the idea. As Nietzsche pointed out, today—in the Vatican— people bow down to a Jewish leader in Rome.

Q. How did you first encounter the Odin Brotherhood?

A. I first met a member of the Brotherhood in a bookshop in

Scotland. I was searching for a volume on a certain secret society—symbolized by a red rose nailed to a cross—when a stranger initiated a conversation. The experience was, I believe, what Karl Jung called a "meaningful coincidence."

Q. In the epilogue of your book, you describe meeting a mysterious eastern European. Can you provide any additional details about the man?

A. I can say he was a university professor, and he was a colorful character. His favorite drink—a kind of mead— he made himself. When I inquired about the recipe, he said" "honey, mixed with spices, is swished around the mouths of pretty girls, and then allowed to ferment."

Q. Did you taste the mead?

A. No, I did not.

Q. And what first interested you in the movement?

A. Several factors. Most of all, however, I was intrigued by the Odinist notion that the gods often visit the planet Earth. The Christian god appears to be a god of the dead. He is seen only by dead people—one sees him in a tunnel of light when one dies—but the living never see his face.

Q. Nietzsche said god is dead. Can you be certain the Odinist gods are not dead?

A. According to legend, the dead cannot laugh. According to the *Eddaic Verses*, Odinist gods often show joy and mirth.

Q. Do not all gods laugh?

A. The God of Judaism seems to laugh with derision in the

second Psalm of the Old Testament, but the New Testament god of guilt and atonement only weeps.

Q. Have you ever seen a god?

A. Not everyone has to see a god. No man has ever seen an atom, but we believe atoms exist.

Q. But have you seen a god? In person?

A. I will have to cite Lao-Tzu—the Chinese sage— on that question. He said "he who tells does not know, and he who knows does not tell."

Q. On the Earth, where is the best place to see a god?

A. Some Odinists have told me that the god Tyr is fond of Germany—Thor is fond of Russia—and I know the Greeks claimed that the goddess Demeter preferred Sicily to Olympus—but I can make no other recommendations..

Q. What about America? Do the Gods visit the United States?

A. I suspect modern America is not favored by the gods. In America, obesity kills more men than war, and fornication is more fertile than marriage.

Q. If one encounters a god, how can the god be recognized?

A. There are traditions about their appearance—in daylight, for example—the gods cast no dark shadow on the Earth— but in most encounters by their wisdom you will know them.

Q. And can you share some wisdom that you were given? Wisdom that does not appear in your book?

A. I was once told that the way of destiny is ruthless. When the autumn comes, no leaf is spared because of its beauty—no flower because of its fragrance.

Q. There are reports that your book on the Odin Brotherhood contains a "skip code." That is, if an adept skips through the book, and reads every fifth, or ninth, or whatever word, there are hidden messages. Is that true?

A. Anything is possible. Consider, however, that a skip code may go in any direction.

Q. How does one join the Odin Brotherhood?

A. The initiation ritual—called "The-Sojourn-of-the Brave—is detailed in the book I wrote. It involves making lesions on the body with a dagger. The ceremony is based on the "marking with the spear" that Snorri Sturluson described.

Q. Why is bloodshed necessary?

A. The ancients believed that rituals need blood to be effective. Julian, the last pagan emperor of Rome, made that point.

Q. Are you a member of the Odin Brotherhood?

A. In the Pacific—in the islands of Micronesia—there is an interesting legend. On the day a man reveals all his secrets—he dies.

So regarding that question, I must remain mysterious.

Q. Are you a member?

A. In the interest of life, I will keep some secrets.

Q. Publicly, you go to great lengths to deny any connection to the Brotherhood. Why is that?

A. I am a simple messenger. The messenger must not be confused with the message.

Q. One final question, Professor Mirabello. In your opinion, what will be the greatest challenge to Odinists in the future?

A. In my opinion, Islam will be the bane of the heathens. The Koran—the infallible word of God for one billion people—a book that believers believe must be obeyed—issues this command: "Fight and kill the pagans wherever you find them...."

The preceding interview was conducted for *Odin Lives* on May 22, 2004. A special thanks to Miss Jennifer Phillips.

Secret Societies: A Brief Essay

By Mark Mirabello, Ph.D.
Professor of History
Shawnee State University

"Secret Societies" are conspiracies working covertly to achieve a hidden agenda. For members, secrecy is a sanctuary and a source of power.

Secret societies often claim to be ancient and they claim direct "initiatory descent" from a fabled founder or group of founders. By definition, no secret society can appear to be a novelty.

Thus, the Brotherhood of the Rose Cross claims direct descent from the mysterious Christian Rosenkreuz (1378 - 1484) and the Odin Brotherhood claims that it was established in 1421.

Critics view "Secret Societies" as malevolent organizations working against the general interests of mankind. They are sometimes outlawed, and the United Kingdom passed the Unlawful Societies Act of 1799 which was the first statue "for the more effectual suppression of societies established for seditious and treasonable purposes." This law was in effect until 1967.

PURPOSES OF SECRET SOCIETIES

Secret societies have various functions, usually esoteric, political, or charitable in nature. Secret societies may plot world domination, subvert legal or financial institutions, enlighten the world, distribute charity, protect a secret, or "attempt to rewrite history by circulating certain literature."

ON SECRECY

To keep anything completely secret is impossible. As the poet Ibn Qutayba (A.D. 828 - 889) lamented, not only does a man disappear after death; his secrets are spread abroad.

Colonel Wendell Fetig, commander of the Filipino-American forces behind Japanese lines in World War II, made this observation about secrecy: "It is almost impossible to maintain but often can be better achieved through the use of misleading rumors than through tight security."

To protect themselves, however, many secret societies use the "Double Blind." In the "double blind" the truth is revealed on the assumption the public will not believe it. When details of the Majestic-12 conspiracy (an alleged government UFO group established after the Roswell "incident") were revealed, conspirators claimed a double blind ruse had been implemented. The Priory of Zion, the Brotherhood of the Rose Cross, the Odin Brotherhood, and the Illuminati allegedly employ this deception.

If anyone does reveal their secret, most secret societies will discredit the informant. According to one interesting and diabolical theory, "the psychological classification of paranoia" has been INVENTED by conspirators (the hidden powers that control the world) for the purpose of discrediting anyone who attempts to expose them.

TYPES OF SECRET SOCIETIES

Generally speaking, there are six types of secret societies.

1) In the first type, the existence of the group is known and the membership is public knowledge, but the rituals and the meetings are secret. This describes the Freemasons.

2) In the second type, the membership and the objectives are public knowledge, but all meetings are private. This describes the Bilderberg Group.

3) In the third type, the existence of the group is known, but the membership and the objectives of the organization are secret. This describes the Hellfire Club.

4) In the fourth type, the existence of the group is rumored, but few, if any, concrete facts are known about the group. This describes the Illuminati.

5) In the fifth type, the existence of the group is rumored, the identities of the members are secret, but the rituals and the objectives are known. This describes the Odin Brotherhood.

6) In the sixth type, the existence of the group is denied, but the identities of the members and the objectives of the group are known. This describes the Mafia.

INITIATION

Admittance into a secret society begins with an initiation ritual. Often, this involves darkness, blindfolds, blood oaths, and symbolic icons such as skulls, daggers, and sacred texts. The candidate undergoes some kind of ordeal, often a symbolic death and resurrection.

According to historian Ronald Hutton, initiation in the Society of the Horseman's Word involves reading the Bible backwards three times over three years, indulging in a mock Eucharist (with bread, jam, and whiskey), and—at the climax of the initiation—"shaking the devil's hand." On the last point, the blindfolded initiate had to grasp a heated spade.

Initiation into the Odin Brotherhood–which only occurs at the solstices—involves a kind of vision quest cemented by a "ceremony of blood." The rite involves solitude, a diet of bread and ice, a white shroud, a dagger, and a fire.

The initiate –after proper purification– makes three incisions on his body. Done in the name of "holy violence, necessary violence," the male neophyte makes three incisions on his chest.

He then "devotes, hallows, and sanctifies" his soul to the "gods who live" by penetrating a fire three times with a dagger stained with his own blood.

The scars are called "The-Marks-of-Joy." They are based on the "marking with the spear ceremony described in the *Ynglinga Saga* by Snorri Sturluson.

The female neophyte, however, makes three small incisions

on the tip of her right index finger. The Odin Brotherhood believes the female's breasts—"the last and most beautiful embellishment she receives in life"—must not be disfigured.

Mercia Eliade, in *Shamanism: Archaic Techniques of Ecstasy*, notes that secret society initiations resemble shamanic initiations, and include seclusion (symbolizing the "beyond), some sort of prohibition (as in a diet), covering the face and body, usually with something that is white, and a difficult ordeal, which involves the infliction of "cruelties."

Many secret societies will have layers of membership, with a person entering first as a neophyte of some sort, and then advancing through the ranks as he participates more in the organization. These ranks are very often called "degrees". Some organizations have as few as one or three degrees, others as many as thirty-three.

As the applicant advances through the ranks, he will often learn new passwords, hand grips, or other modes of recognition during the rituals.

INITIATION RITUALS OF DANGEROUS SECRET SOCIETIES

In the most dangerous secret societies, the initiation ritual requires new members to commit an atrocity that will make them odious to society.

The crime binds participants more closely to the outlaw group, forcing them to share a hateful secret that puts them beyond the pale of humanity. Outcasts–pariahs—they can never rejoin the ordinary collective.

Thus, in magical conventicles, initiates are required to commit brother-sister, father-daughter, or mother-son incest.

To join the Leopard Men of Africa, initiates must provide a daughter or niece for a cannibal-murder feast.

To qualify as a "soldier" in the Mafia (a full member), the individual must have killed at least one man. To complete the initiation, the soldier-to-be pierces his finger—rubs blood on the paper image of a saint—burns the image—takes the ashes in his hand—and swears this oath:

I swear to be loyal to my brothers, never to betray them, always to aid them, and if I fail may I burn and be turned to ashes like the ashes of this image.

According to reports, to join some American outlaw groups the initiates must commit murder and—in front of members of the chapter—they must have sexual intercourse with an underage girl, an elderly woman, and a corpse.

In the Aryan Brotherhood (or Aryan Nation)—America's most dangerous prison organization—the rule is "blood in, blood out." Men become members by committing murder, and they may leave the group only with their own deaths.

The most famous outlaw initiation in history was described by Sallust, the Roman historian who left a written account of the "Catiline Conspiracy." These are Sallust's words:

> There was a rumor current at the time that when Catiline, on the conclusion of his speech, called on the associates of his plot to swear an oath, he passed around bowls of human blood mixed with wine; and

when all had tasted of it after invoking a curse upon themselves if they broke faith, in accordance with the usual practice at such solemn ceremonies, he revealed the details of his scheme. This he is said to have done in order that the consciousness of having jointly participated in such an abomination might make them more loyal to one another.

DEATH OATHS

Some secret societies, such as Propaganda Due, include death oaths in their initiation process.

Licio Gelli, a P2 founder, instructed members to commit suicide with the drug digitalis—provided by the organization—if they were pressured to reveal secrets.

In the absence of an autopsy, a fatal dose of the drug digitalis would be indistinguishable from a heart attack.

SOME REPRESENTATIVE SECRET SOCIETIES:

ORDER OF THE ASSASSINS

The Order of Assassins–known also as the Order of Devoted Masters of the Quiet Death—was organized by Hasan-bin-Sabbah, who was born in 1034 in Iran.

Hasan was one of the founders of asymmetric warfare. He discarded orthodox war–war, he believed, was wasteful–and he used assassination instead. Hasan's Order targeted leaders, either killing them or (more commonly) threatening them with death unless they complied.

According to one Assassin poem:

> By one single warrior on foot a king may be stricken with terror, though he own more than a hundred thousand horsemen.

The elite killers of Hasan's Order were masters of disguise, treachery, and murder. Sent against kings, religious leaders, and military commanders, the killers were deployed alone or in pairs. They infiltrated the enemy's palace—usually as service staff.

The assassins used the "Doctrine of Intelligent Dissimulation." That is to say, they pretended to be something they were not. Lying allowed them to move close to their targets.

The two assassins who killed Conrad of Montferrat—for example—let themselves be baptized as Christians. While praying, they were able to move close to Conrad and assassinate him.

Famous for their patience, members of the Order waited—sometimes for years—until the opportunity was right. Then they struck suddenly. Their favorite weapon was the poisoned dagger.

Always, members of the Order made no attempt to escape. Nor was any effort made to rescue them. They were effective because these pious assassins wanted to die in order to kill.

Little is known about the secrets of the Order. According to

Christian accounts, the assassins had three grades of initiation. Interestingly, the teaching of each level negated anything that had been previously taught. The innermost secret–it was alleged–is that heaven and hell are the same, all actions are indifferent, and there is no good or evil.

The actual assassins–members who had attained the highest degree–were taught that there is no such thing as belief. All that matters is action.

"Nothing is true," taught Hasan, and "all is permitted."

BEATI PAOLI

A secret Sicilian group of black-robed and black-hooded vigilantes, the Beati Paoli defended ordinary citizens from the tyranny of the state and the church. Meeting in secret and plotting vengeance, members were silent killers who stabbed and strangled powerful people who oppressed ordinary people.

Today, the Mafia claims descent from the Beati Paoli.

The Beati Paoli operated at night from their refuge in the catacombs and tunnels under the city of Palermo. These tunnels, called the Grotto of Beati Paoli, may be entered through a house in Palermo. Another entrance is via the valley of the Orphans.

The Beati Paoli kept no records. Like the Druids, all important information was kept only in the human memory.

Described in fiction several times, the best known novel is by Luigi Natoli. Writing under the pen name William Galt, his novel *I Beati Paoli* was published in 1909. The book was later made into a film called *The Black Masked Knights.*

BLACK HAND

The Black Hand was a secret society of Serb assassins, formed in 1911 as the Order of Death. Its purpose was to use assassination to liberate Serbian lands held by other nations.

Organized by Colonel Dragutin Dmitrievich, a Serbian army officer who used the code name "Apis," the Black Hand recruited young people who were dying from terminal diseases.

Initiation involved a dark, candlelit room and a table holding a skull, a pistol, a bomb, and a vial of poison. Initiates were told to place a hand on the skull and to repeat the oath of the Black Hand:

> By the sun that warms me, by the Earth that feeds me,
> by God, by the blood of my ancestors, by my honor
> and life, I swear fidelity to the cause of Serbian
> nationalism, and to sacrifice my life for it.

The most famous member of the Black Hand is Gavrilo Princip (1894-1918). The most influential assassin in history, Gavrilo Princip was nineteen years of age when he sparked World War I by firing two shots—with a pistol—and killed an heir to the Austrian throne.

Princep swallowed cyanide after the attack, but the poison was too old and it failed to kill him. Seized by military officers, their abuse caused Princep to lose an arm.

Too young for the death penalty (at that time reserved for people twenty-one years or older), Princip was sentenced to twenty years. He died in 1918 from tuberculosis.

Honored as a hero by the Serbs, the Gavrilo Princip Museum is dedicated to his memory. The museum preserves Princip's "Black Hand Oath" in his own handwriting:

BROEDERBOND

The Afrikaner Broederbond, a nationalist secret society, grew up among Afrikaners after their defeat in the Boer War in 1902.

Founded in 1918, after the "Century of Wrong," a 1964 study found it had 6,768 members in 473 local divisions. Membership was restricted to white, Afrikaans - speaking males, who were Protestants over the age of twenty-five. Freemasons were not permitted in the group.

In the initiation ceremony, the new member pledged not to divulge his membership or that of others. He promised not to disclose anything about the Bond's discussions, decisions, or activities. He also pledged to serve the Afrikaner nation.

In 1948 the Broederbond helped elevate a white-supremacy movement—the Nationalist Party—to a position of power.

ILLUMINATI

A fabled secret society, the Illuminati were established on May 1, 1776. Originally called the Order of Perfectibilists, the group was organized in Ingolstadt, Bavaria, the place where the fictional Frankenstein created his monster.

The founder of the Illuminati was Adam Weishaupt, a law professor at Ingolstadt University. He used the code name "Spartacus," in honor of the famous rebel slave.

Educated by the Roman Catholic Jesuits, Weishaupt was accepted into Freemasonry in 1774. He would recruit the Illumanti from the Freemasons. The Illuminati members took an oath vowing perpetual silence, unshakable loyalty, and submission to the order.

The Illuminati established the model of a secret society run by leaders who hide the true purposes from the general membership. Known as "double doctrine," the rank and file learn "anodyne" goals, while "unknown superiors" know the organization's true, and quite different, inner secrets.

According to their enemies, the alleged goal of the Illuminati is to destroy Christianity and all world governments. They will then unite everyone under one world government whose ruler is Lucifer.

Others allege that the Illuminati want a utopian "super state" and the abolition of private property, social authority, and nationality. They allegedly favor free love, universal brotherhood, peace, equality, and feminism. They are anti-king and anti-church.

According to Robert Shea and Robert Anton Wilson, however, the Illuminati are "too sophisticated, ruthless, and decadent to want to take over the world." Instead, "it amuses them to play with the world."

KNIGHTS OF THE APOCALYPSE

The Knights of the Apocalypse—a secret society which is only rumored to exist—is an outlaw group. Composed of fiercely pious Roman Catholics, the group was allegedly established in 1693.

Members of the group are assassins. Their mission is to save mankind. Whenever the Anti-Christ is born, they hunt Satan's child and murder him in the cradle. Allegedly, they have killed several children already.

KU KLUX KLAN

Called America's "most persistent terrorist organization," the Ku Klux Klan was established in 1865 by six confederate veterans in Pulaski, Tennessee.

The original Klan was an underground resistance movement to restore white supremacy. Members had to swear an oath of secrecy about Klan activities and the identities of other Klansmen.

Nahan Bedford Forrest, a confederate cavalry leader, was elected "Grand Wizard" of the Klan in 1867. The phrase "Invisible Empire," which referred to the territories where the Klan existed, was coined at the same time.

The original Klan was dormant for a time, but in 1905 Thomas Dixon, Jr. published a novel called *The Clansman: An Historical Romance of the Ku Klux Klan*. Dixon's novel depicted the Klan as an order of chivalry devoted to saving "the South."

The novel inspired D.W. Griffith's film, *The Birth of a Nation*, and the film and book led to the revival of the Klan in 1915.

President Woodrow Wilson, after viewing the film, claimed that the K.K.K. had saved civilization on the North American continent.

President Warren Harding, Wilson's successor, was initiated into the Klan in the Green Room of White House. Supreme Court Justice Hugo Black joined the Klan in the 1920's.

Also, a young Harry Truman paid a ten-dollar initiation fee to the Missouri K.K.K.

At the end of the twentieth century, however, the Ku Klux Klan changed.

In 1983, Robert Miles, a Ku Klux Klan leader, claimed that the organization had to revert to its original form as a military underground operating in "enemy-controlled territory."

According to Miles, the Klan could no longer support the police or the American Constitution because hostile forces control both.

Also in 1983, Louis Beam, in his "Essays of a Klansman," said that for the third time in the history of the United States the government is the enemy of the people. The other two times, he claimed, were 1776 and 1861.

Beam said that resistance should come from decentralized cadres, like the Minutemen in 1776 and the original Klan. He claimed that 1776 was not a popular uprising—it was an "unpopular rebellion of a politically radical minority."

SOCIETY OF THE LEOPARD

Centered in West Africa, in Sierra Leone, the Society of the Leopard is an ancient secret society of men who hunt humans.

To join the Society of the Leopard, initiates must provide a young girl for sacrifice. The victim, who has to be the initiate's own sister or daughter, is murdered with a claw knife.

Members of the society always kill at night, wearing leopard skins over the body and pronged, claw-like weapons with double-edged blades over the hands. The leopard is their totem, and they practice rites involving cannibalism and blood drinking to gain magic power.

When not hunting, the Leopard Society members live an otherwise normal existence. Like the Thuggee of India, they are sworn to secrecy.

On August 5, 1895, the British executed three Leopard men for murdering travelers. One of the Leopard men had been a Christian Sunday School teacher.

LUDDITES

Established in 1811, the Luddites were a secret society (with oaths and passwords) dedicated to destroying the machines of the industrial age that were causing human unemployment.

The Luddite attackers operated at night, wore masks, and used hand tools to smash the machinery destroying jobs. The group took its name from a semi-mythical worker in Leicester who destroyed machinery.

In 1812, the British government introduced the death penalty for breaking machines. Note that the governing class valued a machine over a human life!

MAFIA

A form of organized crime, the Mafia is the most secret and most powerful of all secret societies. First referred to in a play from 1862, only members can be certain of its existence.

The fact that a man is a member can never be admitted. At most, the member allows himself to be called a "man of respect" or a "friend of friends." The Mafia has no secret handshakes or passwords, but a member can be recognized because he will have spectacular success in all of his endeavors. The Mafia lawyer will win all of his cases—the Mafia physician will draw all of the patients—the mafia businessman will never lose money.

The defining feature of the classic Sicilian Mafia is the concept of *Omerta*. The word literally means "manliness," and *Omerta* obliges a man to be strong, to be potent, and to dominate.

More precisely, *omerta* means silence and self-restraint. If wronged, the "man of respect" will not show anger, he will not tell the police, and he will not act rashly. He will wait—for years if necessary—and avenge in the coldest way possible, often striking when he seems to be the victim's friend.

ODIN BROTHERHOOD

A mysterious "Odinist" organization (one dedicated to preserving the lore and virtues of the gods and goddesses of the Norse pantheon, as described in the *Eddaic Verses*), the Odin Brotherhood to have been established in 1421, after a necromantic ceremony.

Initiation, which involves bread and ice, a dagger, a fire, and markings on the flesh, is conducted only during the solstices. Women as well as men are found in the movement.

Unlike most secret societies, the Odin Brotherhood is non-hierarchical. Members, who initiate themselves after receive a calling in a dream-vision, belong to a "conspiracy of equals."

In terms of eschatology, the Odin Brotherhood teaches that "nothing dies forever." Death is inevitable, but from death comes new life.

ORDER OF SKULL AND BONES

"The Order," which is also called Chapter 322, and was once known as the "Brotherhood of Death," is called "Skull and Bones" by those who make light of it. A mysterious secret society, it was founded in 1833 at Yale University by Huntington Russell (an opium trader) and Alphonso Taft (an ancestor of the president).

The emblem of the Order is the Death's Head, or two crossed bones and a skull. Its headquarters, called the "tomb," is a dark, windowless building. There are claims that the Order possesses the skulls of Geronimo, Pancho Villa, and Martin Van Buren—all stolen.

According to Anthony C. Sutton, the author of *America's Secret Establishment*, no one can ask to join Skull and Bones, which admits only fifteen new members each year. Membership is by invitation only.

Allegedly, the Order does not want loners, iconoclasts, or individualists in the organization. They want amoral team players—people who will sacrifice themselves for the group.

According to Sutton, the initiation of new members involves some nudity. The initiate is placed in a coffin—he is carried to the center of the building—he is chanted over—and his name is inscribed in a bone.

New members are called knights. After one year, they are then called patriarchs. They will be called patriarchs the rest of their lives. The Order refers to all outsiders as vandals.

The patriarchs of the Order meet annually, on the oddly spelled "Deer Iland," in the St. Lawrence River, in New York.

Members are sworn to silence. They are forbidden to discuss the organization, its procedures, or its objectives. Words spoken within the Order may not be written—even in letters to fellow members.

Members must always deny membership to outsiders. If the Order is under discussion, members may not remain in the room.

The function of the Order is to bring about certain mysterious objectives. Honors and financial awards are guaranteed, and initiates are assured career advancement–success—even wealth.

THUGGEE

The Thuggee—an ancient cult of murder and terror—have been called "the most successful terror organization in history" and "the most remarkable example of organized crime on record." Allegedly extinct, there are reports that they still exist today.

The Thuggee are devotees of Kali, the Hindu goddess of death. Kali is depicted as black-skinned, with four arms. In her first hand she carries a sword, in her second hand she carries a severed head, her third hand is raised in a gesture of peace, and her remaining hand is grasping for power. The city of Calcutta is named in her honor.

According to legend, the first Thuggee were created (from the brow of the goddess) to help Kali destroy a horde of demons. The demons had to be strangled, for their blood— once shed—turned into more demons. So Kali gave the Thuggee the noose to kill demons.

In return for helping Kali, the Thuggee believe that they received the right to kill in perpetuity and to keep the loot from their victims. They are obliged to strangle at least one person per year. The victim must never be a woman or a wandering holy man.

The Thuggee believe that their victims go straight to paradise. By serving Kali, the Thuggee also go to paradise.

The word Thug (pronounced t'ug) is derived from the Sanskrit word which means deceiver or swindler. Members of this secret cult lead double lives. For most of the year, the Thuggee have regular employment and live openly in the community as respected and orderly citizens.

In autumn, however, when the roads are crowded with pilgrims, the Thuggee hunt humans. They attack in November and December—always at least one hundred miles from their homes. When the killing season ends, they melt back into ordinary life.

The Thuggee work in units of ten to fifty men. Divided into small groups, some serve as scouts, some as killers, and some as grave diggers.

The Thuggee strangle their selected victims, using garrotes fashioned from white or yellow silk. (White and yellow are sacred to Kali.) The agony of the victim is prolonged because Kali enjoys terror.

Usually, there are three Thuggee killers per victim. While one strangles, one holds the dying man's feet, and one holds the arms or sits on the chest of the victim.

After the killings, the victims are buried in small, deep graves, with their backs and thigh bones broken. To hide the activity, the graves are dug inside tents.

The graves are dug with shovels and at least one symbolic strike from a silver pick axe. The site is strewn with pungent herbs to mislead dogs.

The Thuggee always conduct an ancient ceremony on the

graves. They place "goor," a kind of coarse sugar, on a cloth. After pouring some sugar and "holy water," those that had killed that day (in order of seniority) eat the "sugar of Kali" as a sacrament. It is said that once a man tastes goor, he will always serve the goddess of death.

To perpetuate the movement, men recruit their sons and nephews. The training of the boys begins in childhood, but only at the age of eighteen are the boys allowed to kill and taste the sacred sugar for the first time.

SELECT BIBLIOGRAPHY

Axelrod, Alan. *The International Encyclopedia of Secret Societies and Fraternal Orders.*

Baigent, Michael, Leigh, Richard, and Lincoln, Henry. *Holy Blood, Holy Grail.*

Barrett. David V. *Secret Societies. From the Ancient and Arcane to the Modern and Clandestine.*

Beatty, Kenneth J. *Human Leopards.*

Butt-Thompson, F.W. *West African Secret Societies.*

David-Neel, Alexandra. *Magic and Mystery in Tibet.*

Daroul, Arkon. *A History of Secret Societies.*

Dixon, Thomas. *The Clansman: An Historical Romance of the Ku Klux Klan.*

Epperson, A Ralph. *The Unseen Hand.*

Estulin, Daniel. *The True Story of the Bilderberg Group.*

Froude, James Anthony. *The Knights Templar.*

Grayson, Cameron. *Prehistoric Secret Societies: The Origin of Clandestine Communities.*

Hall, Manly Palmer. *Rosicrucian and Masonic Origins.*

Hall, Manly Palmer. *The Secret Teachings of All Ages.*

Heckethorn, Charles. *The Secret Societies of all Ages and Countries, Embracing the Mysteries of Ancient India, China, Japan, Egypt, Mexico, Peru, Greece, and Scandinavia, the Cabbalists, early*

Christians, heretics, Assassins, Thugs, Templars, the Vehm and Inquisition, Mystics, Rosicrucians, Illuminati, Freemasons, Skopzi, Camorristi, Carbonari, Nihilists, and other Sects.

Hitti, Philip K. *Origins of the Druze People and Religion.*

Hodapp, Christopher and Von Kannon, Alice. *Conspiracy Theories & Secret Societies For Dummies.*

Howard, Michael. *Secret Societies: Their Influence and Power from Antiquity to the Present Day.*

Huffman, Michael A. *Secret Societies and Psychological Warfare.*

Jones, Bernard E. *Freemasons' Guide and Compendium.*

Joseph, Isya. *Devil Worship: The Sacred Books and Traditions of the Yezidiz.*

Keightley, Thomas. *Secret Societies of the Middle Ages.*

Klimczuk, Stephen and Warner, Gerald. *Secret Places, Hidden Sanctuaries: Uncovering Mysterious Sights, Symbols, and Societies.*

Kreyenbroek, Philip G. *Yezidism-Its Background, Observances and Textual Tradition.*

Lewis, Bernard. *The Assassins.*

Lewis, Jon E. Mammoth Book of Cover-Ups.

Lewis, Norman. *The Honored Society.*

Lord, Evelyn. *The Hellfire Clubs: Sex, Satanism and Secret Societies.*

Lung, Haha. *Ancient Art of Strangulation.*

Marrs, Jim. *Rule by Secrecy: The Hidden History That Connects the Trilateral Commission, the Freemasons, and the Great Pyramids.*

McBrewster, John (Editor), Miller, Frederic P. (Editor), and Vandome, Agnes F. (Editor). *Strategy of Tension: Piazza Fontana bombing, Bologna Massacre, False Flag, Propaganda Due, Licio Gelli, 1980 Turkish Coup D'état, Enrico Mattei, Gladio in Italy, Disinformation.*

MacKenzie, David. *Violent Solutions: Revolutions, Nationalism, and Secret Societies in Europe to 1918.*

Mirabello, Mark. *The Odin Brotherhood.*

Mirabello, Mark. *Handbook for Rebels and Outlaws.*

Morgan, William. *Morgan's Freemasonry Exposed and Explained: Showing the Origin, History and Nature of Masonry; Its Effects on the Government, and the Christian Religion.*

Newton, Michael. *The Ku Klux Klan: History, Organization, Language, Influence And Activities of America's Most Notorious Secret Society.*

Prichard, Samuel. *Masonry Dissected.*

Reynolds, John Lawrence. *Secret Societies: Inside the World's Most Notorious Organizations.*

Roberts, John Morris. *The Mythology of the Secret Societies.*

Serfontein, J.H.P. *Brotherhood of Power: An Expose of the Secret Afrikaner Broederbond.*

Shea, Robert and Wilson, Robert Anton. *The Illuminatus! Trilogy: The Eye in the Pyramid, The Golden Apple, Leviathan.*

Sora, Steven. *Secret Societies of America's Elite: From the Knights Templar to Skull and Bones.*

Streeter, Michael. *Behind Closed Doors.*

Sutton, Anthony. *America's Secret Establishment: An Introduction to the Order of Skull & Bones.*

Vivian, Herbert. *Secret Societies Old and New.*

Waite, Arthur Edward *The Real History of the Rosicrucians: Founded on their own Manifestoes, and on Facts and Documents Collected from the Writings of Initiated Brethren.*

Waite, Arthur Edward. *Complete Rosicrucian Initiations of the Fellowship of the Rosy Cross.*

Webster, Hutton. *Primitive Secret Societies.*

Yates, Frances. *The Rosicrucian Enlightenment.*

War, Odin, and Valhalla

War is normal in the human experience. In the past 3400 years, according to Chris Hedges, 'humans have been entirely at peace for *268* of them."

Of all warriors, as the great religious scholar Joseph Campbell pointed out, some of the hardiest are the nomadic pastoralists. Unlike the farmer, who wants a fixed roof and regular meals, the pastoral nomad is constantly moving through hostile terrain with his herds. The nomad eats and drinks when he can, braves all weathers, and is grateful for small mercies.

Accustomed to a life of dominating animals and butchering them with his own hands, the pastoral nomad lives a life based on force and blood.

Indeed, the pastoral nomad's ferocity can shock modern ethicists. Mistreating subordinates causes outrage today, but the Scythians, as Herodotus noted, blinded *all* of their slaves to make them more manageable.

Along with the Zulus of Africa, and the Mongols of Asia, perhaps the elite fighters of all such wanderers were the so-called "Aryans" (from the Sanskrit *Arya*, which means "noble"). The "Aryans," now typically called Indo-Europeans, were ancient nomads who inhabited the vast arid steppe (derived from the Russian word for "wasteland") that stretches 5,000 kilometers across Eurasia. Described by Carroll Quigley as patriarchal, warlike, horse-loving, sky-worshipping, and honor-seeking warriors, the Indo-Europeans viewed the "good life" as consisting of strong sons, swift horses, and fat cows. Through force of arms, according to Marija Gimbutas, these fierce people established themselves as a ruling class over the peaceful, earth-loving, fertility-dominated, female-oriented peasants.

The Indo-Europeans moved vast distances (significantly, the *Prose Edda* notes that Odin, Vili, and Ve made humans from *driftwood* on the shore), and, thanks to the discoveries of an eighteenth-century scholar named Sir William Jones, we now know that the descendents of these Indo-Europeans today speak the Celtic, Germanic, Italic, Baltic, Slavic, Albanian, Hellenic, Armenian, and Indo-Iranian tongues.

Like all warriors, these Indo-Europeans had an ethical system based on honor and shame, rather than guilt and sin. In a shame culture, the highest good is public esteem—in contrast to a guilt culture, where the highest good is a quiet conscience.

In such an honor culture, reputation is everything. Thus, in the Norse *Hávamál*, these words are uttered:

Cattle die, kindred die,

Every man is mortal:

But I know one thing that never dies,

The glory of the great deed.

In an honor/shame society, men are charged with maintaining their own honor and that of their women. (As Margaret Clunies Ross has pointed out, female honor is largely defined in terms of approved sexual behavior.)

In all cases, in a shame society a man responds to aspersions on honor with physical violence or an act designed to humiliate the offender.

These Indo-Europeans are described in great detail in the ancient *Vedas* of Hinduism. Although the *Vedas* are the scriptures of the Hindus, the religion *in* the *Vedas* is quite different from modern Hinduism.

The *Vedas* contain no yoga, no pacifism, and no vegetarianism. The "Aryas" in the *Vedas* slaughtered cows for meat and flayed them for leather.

The Vedas describe a polygamous and patriarchal people who were proud of their genealogies. Addicted to intoxicating substances and gambling, they were tent dwellers who were tough and warlike.

Curiously, according *Rig Veda* 7.21.5, the invading *Aryas* called the native population of India "devils" (*dasas, dasyus*) "whose god is the phallus" (*sisna-deva*).

At death, the *Vedic* Aryas were *not* absorbed into the "absolute." Instead, after the eldest son performed a special set of post-cremation rituals (called *sapindikarana*), the dead man would journey to the "World of the Fathers."

Another group of Indo-Europeans were the Germanic peoples, who moved north, instead of south, as the Vedic Aryans had done. Famous for their "desire of fame and contempt for death," their leader was a tribal chief named Odin (also called Woden and Wotan). Described by Edward Gibbon as a warrior and a magician, Odin was the leader of a tribe in Sarmatia, and he led his people to Sweden.

At the end, wrote Gibbon, Odin performed a death rite and wounded himself in "nine mortal places."

The *Ynglinga Saga*, written by Snorri Sturluson, provides us with additional details. According to Sturluson, Odin spoke only in verse, he could make his enemies blind, deaf, or afraid, he could shape-shift, he could place his body in a trance while he wandered in animal form, and he could work *seid* magic.

Although depicting Odin as a man appears to simple euhemerism—it is not. All ancient gods, according to the legends, once walked the earth. Indeed, as Sir James Frazer pointed out, the aboriginal people of central Australia, perhaps the oldest human culture on the planet, did *not* have gods; instead, they revered their ancestors, and they believed that these ancestors were continuously reborn as descendants. And so, it should not surprise us that one could visit the mummified head of Osiris in Abydos in ancient Egypt, or that, as Pausanias, the ancient Greek writer, noted, one could view the grave of Zeus in ancient Crete.

These "elders" had graves—but still they lived.

But, if Odin exists, where is he now? Note that the Norse universe is a series of self-contained domains, the so-called "Nine Worlds," and that each of these domains is reachable only by a protracted effort. To a people who lived in world of fjords and islands, and seas, mountains, and glaciers, the logic of this model of the universe was obvious.

So, where is Odin? Although he sometimes visits the world of men (the *Heimskringla* tells how Odin visited the court of King Olaf Tryggrason), and he sometimes visits the realm of the Frost Giants (*Vafthruthnismol* details how Odin made a death wager with a wise troll), Odin's normal habitation is Asgard, the stronghold of the Norse gods, where he presides over fabled Valhalla, the hall of the heroic slain. Thatched with golden shields, accessed by hundreds of doors, Valhalla is the most magnificent of all structures.

Unlike the Christian heaven, which is a gift for a life lived (the "faithful" who kneel, believe, and obey), Odin's Valhalla is earned by the *mode* of death. Specifically, Odin's Valhalla is open to intrepid warriors who die heroic deaths.

Linking the method of death with the afterlife is found in many cultures—the combative Aztecs, for example, promised a glorious existence with the sun god for warriors who died in battle or who were killed on the stone of sacrifice, and the Aztecs also promised a glorious existence with the sun god for women who died giving birth (the feminine equivalent of death in battle). (Interestingly, in the *Eddaic Grímnismál*, the lovely Freyja takes half of the heroic dead, and this may be a reference to women who die giving birth, as in the Aztec lore. Note that, according to modern global figures, childbirth kills approximately 343,000 women each year and war kills about 378,000 men annually.)

In peaceful urban cultures, a bloody death is viewed as undesirable—city dwellers want a quiet death, a "straw death," a death in bed from old age or sickness—where the soul exits peacefully through the mouth of the dying man. (If the dying man is especially sordid, however, the Jains of India and the Buddhists of Tibet assert that the soul exits through the anus.)

But in a violent death, the treasured death of warriors, the soul exits quickly and cleanly through the gaping wound. About such deaths, the Greek Heraclitus said, ""Souls slain in war are purer than those that perish with disease. They arise into wakefulness…"

In addition to being purer, warlike cultures maintain that the war dead reach the next world in a more vigorous form. Since the soul has the age and appearance of the dead person at the time of death, young men who die here are young men over there. This belief inspired Yukio Mishima, a warrior in the Japanese Bushido tradition, and he committed suicide by *seppuku* in 1970 while still relatively young. According to Mishima, "A powerful, tragic frame and sculptured muscles" are "indispensable in a romantically noble death. Any confrontation between weak, flabby flesh and death seemed to me absurdly inappropriate."

And, of course, since the ancient Germanic peoples were warriors, the ideal Germanic death was a "blood work." The mighty Ragnar Lodbrok, imprisoned by his enemies in a pit filled with squirming snakes, was killed violently by the reptiles. According to his saga, Ragnar Lodbrok spoke these final words:

> I desire my death now.
> The disir call me home,
> whom Herjan hastens onward
> from his hall, to take me.
> On the high bench, boldly,
> I'll drink beer with the Aesir;
> hope of life is lost now,
> laughing shall I die!

Like any warrior culture, however, the Germanic Vikings, knew that sometimes brave men did *not* fall on the field of battle. Midgard, the world of men, is a place of misadventure and plague, so Odin provided a kind of "skeleton key" to Valhalla to his brave acolytes. A special rite, called "marking with the spear," is described in the *Ynglinga Saga,* and the text notes that both Odin himself and the god Njord underwent the procedure. In the words of H. M. Chadwick, the author of *The Cult of Othin,* "the rite was clearly regarded by the writer of *Ynglinga Saga* as a substitution for death in battle."

Among modern pagans, a version of the Odin rite lives on among a group called the Odin Brotherhood. The ritual, which allegedly leads to Valhalla, is conducted by initiates who join the group. Involving solitude, a diet of bread and ice, a white death shroud, wood from a lightning-struck tree, a fire, and three cuts to the flesh, the procedure is conducted once per life, and only at the solstices, a threshold time when supernatural forces seep into this world.

Moreover, when initiated members of the Odin Brotherhood do approach death, they make a wound on the body, so that the soul may escape cleanly and strongly. They are buried standing up—like Hrap in the saga story—together with certain possessions and treasures. (Odin, according to Snorri Sturluson, promised that in the next world a man would "enjoy whatever he himself had buried in the earth.") These possessions are first broken or burned, because just as killing a man dispatches him to the next world, breaking or burning objects conveys them to "the other side."

Now, according to the legends, Odin, the war god, uses his shapely Valkyries to gather the heroic dead to Valhalla, but the heroes are not summoned to vegetate in eternal bliss. (In contrast, in the *only* biblical description of the Christian heaven, found in chapter four of the *Book of Revelation*, the residents spend eternity declaring: "Holy, holy, holy, Lord God Almighty, which was, and is, and is to come.") No, an invitation to enter Valhalla is an honor, but Valhalla is *not* an old soldiers' home. Resembling a barracks for elite forces, Valhalla is a place for the champions to enjoy pork, mead, beer, and women by night, while they indulge in bloody war games by day.

To be summoned to Odin's Valhalla is an honor, but it also a *responsibility*. At the end of *this* universe, in a final battle called Ragnarok, when Odin sallies forth to certain death, his chosen Valhalla champions, called the *Einherjar*, will stand with the gods and will die with them.

In contrast to the Christians, who want to escape this doomed universe in the "rapture" (described in the *First Epistle of Paul to the Thessalonians*), the champions in Valhalla want a glorious doom.

But, if the *Einharejer* die, is that the end for them? The answer, of course, is no. Indo-European destinations (with the exception of the paradise in the Persian *Avesta*) are typically *not* forever. Although death, according to the Indo-Europeans, is inevitable ("All beings are destroyed when their time comes," declares the *Shiva Purana*, "whether they are gods or mosquitoes"), death is not the end. As Krishna says to the warrior prince Arjuna in the *Bhagavad Gîtâ* (verse 19):

If any man thinks he slays, and if another thinks he is

slain, neither knows the way of truth. The Eternal in man cannot kill: the Eternal in man cannot die.

Likewise, in Germanic legend, the end is not the end. Instead, destruction is a form of purification that leads to a new existence.

Indeed, in Germanic lore, as in virtually all Indo-European lore, the universe itself goes through birth, growth, and destruction, followed by rebirth.

This universe, the cosmos which features Odin, the Allfather, the "lord of the spear," will be followed by another universe, this one without Odin, and that universe, which features Balder, the son of Odin, as a leader, will be followed by another different universe.

In the Norse/Germanic legends, no universe is created *ex nihilo*—but each universe seems to emerge from the wreckage of the previous cosmos. This is how the *Prose Edda* describes the emergence of Odin's grandfather at the start of this universe:

> She licked the ice-blocks, which were salty; and the first day that she licked the blocks, there came forth from the blocks in the evening a man's hair; the second day, a man's head; the third day the whole man was there. He is named Búri: he was fair of feature, great and mighty. He begat a son called Borr.

Modern readers, conditioned by Judaic-Christian notions of linear time (which has one beginning, one unique history, and one inevitable end), assume that Buri was *born* in the salty ice block, but, more likely, the grandfather of Odin, a survivor from a previous universe, was *released.*

And, appropriate for a myth that probably originated from pastoral nomads, the "she" that releases Odin's grandfather is a cow.

Now, if universe follows universe, how many will there be? There are at least nine—two books in the *Prose Edda, Gylfaginning* and *Skáldskaparmál,* note that Heimdall is the son of nine mothers, and that suggests nine births and nine lives for the god.

But what of Odin? Will he return?

In Indo-European lore, time curves back upon itself. As the book *Hamlet's Mill* points out, Aristotle, the "master of those who know," said that what is eternal is circular and what is circular is eternal.

In the circle of time—called the "Eternal Return" by Friedrich Wilhelm Nietzsche and the "Great Year" by the Babylonians and the Greeks—all entities return, and all history is repeated exactly.

Augustine, the Christian theologian, believing that the incarnation of Christ was a unique event, denounced the idea of the Eternal Return in *The City of God:* "For Christ died once for our sins, and rising again, does no more."

But, in fact, the Eternal Return may be an inevitable fact. Henri Poincaré, the great scientist, theorized that given enough time, every closed system returns to its initial state, and Louis Auguste Blanqui, another scholar, showed that, given infinite time and infinite space, the eternal return was a mathematical certainty.

And so, in the words of the Odin Brotherhood, "time is an endless circle in which all possible destinies are repeated forever."

Meaning, as Sir Thomas Browne noted in his *Religio Medici* in 1643:

> And in this sense, I say, the world was before the Creation, and at an end before it had a beginning; and thus was I dead before I was alive...

But, of course, both the demise of Odin, and his eventual return, lie deep into the future (and, if there is an eternal return, in the past!). Meanwhile, not knowing when the "Wolf" will come—not knowing when the final battle will occur—Odin calmly and deliberately gathers his warrior host, preparing for Ragnarok.

But, where is Valhalla? Where do the champions gather? No one knows, but the late David Lane, a Wotanist leader, interpreted Valhalla in an interesting fashion. According to Lane, those who "coast" through life without fighting are thralls. At death, they dissolve into an energy chaos without form or thought. This, claimed Lane, is the Helheim or Helgard of the Norse religion, the mysterious realm of Hela.

The warrior, said Lane, goes to Valhalla, where he spends his days in heroic battle—and his nights in the embrace of the Valkyries. But this Valhalla, with its daily battles and many loves, means successive reincarnations on earth. The warrior soul reincarnates again and again for new adventures on Midgard itself.

Very literally, David Lane said Valhalla is *reincarnation on earth to continue the struggle.*

Technically, Lane's interpretation *appears* to contradict *Eddaic* lore—Valhalla is in Asgard, and is not Asgard in the heavens above? Is not Bifrost, the bridge that links Midgard, the world of men, and Asgard, the stronghold of the Aesir, not, as many scholars have argued, the Milky Way, which extends into space?

True, but Bifrost may also be the rainbow, and this rainbow may go from a point on Midgard to a point in the sky, and this point *could* be Mount Kailish, also called Swastika Mountain, the *only* mountain on the planet that has *never been climbed by man.* No one has ever been allowed on the summit of Swastika Mountain because the Hindus, through the ages, have believed that Shiva and his paradise are there. Of course—and this is significant—Shiva is also the god Rudra of the *Vedas,* and distinguished scholars, such as Kris Kershaw, the author of *The One-Eyed God: Odin and the (Indo-) Germanic Männerbünde,* and Wolf-Dieter Storl, the author of *Shiva: The Wild God of Power and Ecstasy* have identified Rudra with Odin.

So, perhaps Odin and his warrior host in Valhalla are closer than we think.

ACKNOWLEDGEMENTS

David W. Anthony. *The Horse, the Wheel, and Language: How Bronze-Age Riders from the Eurasian Steppes Shaped the Modern World.*

Augustine. *The City of God.*

Thomas Barfield. *The Nomadic Alternative.*

The Bhagavad Gita .

Christian Blinkenberg. *The Thunderweapon in Religion and Folklore: A Study in Comparative Archaeology.*

Lois Bragg. *Oedipus Borealis: The Aberrant Body in Old Icelandic Myth and Saga.*

Sir Thomas Browne. *Religio Medici.*

Jesse L. Byock. *Feud in the Icelandic Saga.*

Jesse L. Byock. *Viking Age Iceland.*

Joseph Campbell. *The Masks of God.* 4 volumes.

Friar Giovanni Di Plan Carpini. *The Story of the Mongols Whom We Call the Tartars.*

Hector Munro Chadwick. *The Cult of Othin: an Essay in the Ancient Religion of the North.*

D. E. Martin Clarke. *The Hávamál: With Selections from Other Poems of The Edda, Illustrating the Wisdom of the North in Heathen Times.*

Carlton S. Coon. *The Hunting Peoples.*

Alain Danielou. *The Myths and Gods of India.*

Alain Danielou. *Gods of Love and Ecstasy: The Traditions of Shiva and Dionysus.*

H.R. Ellis Davidson. *Gods and Myths of Northern Europe.*

Wendy Doniger. *The Hindus: An Alternative History.*

Wendy Doniger. *Karma and Rebirth in Classical Indian Traditions.*

Wendy Doniger *The Origins of Evil in Hindu Mythology.*

Wendy Doniger. *Siva: The Erotic Ascetic.*

Abbe J. A. Dubois. *Hindu Manners, Customs and Ceremonies: The Classic First-Hand Account of India in the Early Nineteenth Century.*

Paul Belloni Du Chaillu. *The Viking Age: the Early History, Manners, and Customs of the Ancestors of the English-Speaking Nations.* 2 volumes.

Georges Dumézil. *Gods of the Ancient Northmen.*

Fray Diego Durán. *The History of the Indies of New Spain.*

Mircea Eliade. *History of Religious Ideas.* 3 volumes.

Mircea Eliade. *The Myth of the Eternal Return: Cosmos and History* .

Mircea Eliade. *Shamanism: Archaic Techniques of Ecstasy.*

Hilda R. Ellis. *Road to Hel: Study of the Conception of the Dead in Old Norse Literature.*

Dan Falk. *In Search of Time: The History, Physics, and Philosophy of Time.*

Sir James Frazer. *The Belief in Immortality and the Worship of the Dead.* 3 volumes.

Sir James Frazer. *The Golden Bough.*

Edward Gibbon. *History of the Decline and Fall of the Roman Empire.* 6 vols.

George William Gilmore. *Animism: Or, Thought Currents of Primitive Peoples.*

Marija Gimbutas. *The Language of the Goddess.*

Paddy Griffith. *Viking Art of War.*

Kveldulf Gundarsson. *Our Troth: History and Lore.*

Hans F. K. Gunther. *The Religious Attitudes of the Indo-Europeans.*

Lawrence J. Hatab. *Nietzsche's Life Sentence: Coming to Terms with Eternal Recurrence.*

Jean Haudry. *The Indo-Europeans.*

Chris Hedges. *What Every Person Should Know about War.*

Herodotus. *The Histories.*

Erik Hildinger. *Warriors of the Steppe: A Military History of Central Asia, 500 B.C. to A.D. 1700.*

Homer. *Iliad.*

Sarah Iles Johnston. *Ancient Religions.*

Shapurji Aspaniarji Kapadia. *The Teachings of Zoroaster, and the Philosophy of the Parsi Religion* .

Friedrich Kauffmann *Northern Mythology.*

Lawrence H. Keeley. *War Before Civilization: The Myth of the Peaceful Savage.*

Kris Kersha. *The One-Eyed God: Odin and the (Indo-) Germanic Männerbünde.*

Anatoly M. Khazanov. *Nomads and the Outside World.*

Ian Knight. *The Anatomy of the Zulu Army: From Shaka to Cetshway, 1818-1879.*

David Lane. *Victory Or Valhalla: The Final Compilation Of Writings By David Lane.*

John Lindow. Norse *Mythology: A Guide to Gods, Heroes, Rituals, and Beliefs.*

Bruce Lincoln. *Death, War, and Sacrifice: Studies in Ideology and Practice.*

Robert. H Lowie. *Primitive Religion.*

Karl Löwith. *Nietzsche's Philosophy of the Eternal Recurrence of the Same.*

Ned Lukacher. *Time-Fetishes: The Secret History of Eternal Recurrence.*

Peter McAllister. *Manthropology: The Science of Why the Modern Male Is Not the Man He Used to Be.*

J. A. MacCulloch. *The Celtic and Scandinavian Religions.*

Timothy May. *The Mongol Art of War*

James Mew. *Traditional Aspects of Hell, Ancient and Modern.*

Mark Mirabello. *The Odin Brotherhood*

Mark Mirabello. *Handbook for Rebels and Outlaws.*

Friedrich Max Mueller. *History of Ancient Sanskrit Literature, so far as it Illustrates the Primitive Religion of the Brahmans.*

John Nathan. *Mishima: A Biography.*

Friedrich Nietzsche. *Works of Friedrich Nietzsche.* 8 volumes.

Hiroshi Obayashi . *Death and Afterlife: Perspectives of World Religions.*

Osred. *Odinism: Present, Past And Future.*

The Poetic Edda (Oxford World's Classics) by Carolyne Larrington (Jul 15, 2009)

Bertram S. Puckle. *Funeral Customs.*

Jaan Puhvel. *Comparative Mythology.*

Carroll Quigley. *The Evolution of Civilizations.*

Colin Renfrew. *Archaeology and Language: The Puzzle of Indo-European Origins.*

Lama Lodu Rinpoche. *Bardo Teachings: The Way of Death and Rebirth.*

Spencer Lee Rogers. *Shaman, His Symbols and His Healing Power.*

Margaret Clunies Ross. *Prolonged Echoes: The Myths (The Viking Collection, Studies in Northern Civilization , Vol 7)*.

Saga of the Jomsvikings.

Jayatilal S. Sanghvi. *A Treatise On Jainism*.

Giorgio de Santillana and Hertha von Dechen. *Hamlet's Mill: An Essay Investigating the Origins of Human Knowledge And Its Transmission Through Myth*.

P. D. Chantepie de La Saussaye. *The Religion Of The Teutons*.

Henry Scott-Stokes. *The Life and Death of Yukio Mishima*.

Gregory Shushan and Gavin Flood. *Conceptions of the Afterlife in Early Civilizations: Universalism, Constructivism and Near-Death Experience*.

Rudolf Simek. *Dictionary of Northern Mythology*.

Jacques Soustelle. *Daily Life of the Aztecs*.

Michael Speidel. *Ancient Germanic Warriors: Warrior Styles from Trajan's Column to Icelandic Sagas*.

Martina Sprague. *Norse Warfare: The Unconventional Battle Strategies of the Ancient Vikings*.

Mikhail Ivanovich Steblin-Kamenskii. *Myth: The Icelandic Sagas & Eddas*.

Frank Henderson Stewart. *Honor*.

Wolf-Dieter Storl. *Shiva: The Wild God of Power and Ecstasy*.

Snorri Sturluson. *Heimskringla: History of the Kings of Norway*

Snorri Sturluson. *The Prose Edda.*

Snorri Sturluson. *The Sagas of Olaf Tryggvason and of Harald the Tyrant.*

Snorri Sturluson. *The Ynglinga Saga.*

Tony Swain and Garry Trompf . *The Religions of Oceania.*

Preben Meulengracht Sýrensen. *The Unmanly Man: Concepts of Sexual Defamation in Early Northern Society.*

Tacitus. *Germania.*

Isaac Taylor. *The Origin of The Aryans An Account Of The Prehistoric Ethnology And Civilization Of Europe.*

G. W. Trompf. *Melanesian Religion.*

Edward Oswald Gabriel Turville-Petre . *Myth and Religion of the North: The Religion of Ancient Scandinavia.*

Edward Tylor. *Religion in Primitive Culture.*

The Vedas. Translated F. Max Muller. The Sacred Books of the East. 50 volumes.

John G. Withnell. *The Customs and Traditions of the Aboriginal Natives of North Western Australia.*

Ben Waggoner. *The Sagas of Ragnar Lodbrok.*

M. L. West. *Indo-European Poetry and Myth.*

Edred Wodanson. *Asatru - The Hidden Fortress.*

C. H. Yarrow. *An Introduction to the Mortuary Customs of the North American Indians.*

Also by Mark Mirabello
Handbook for Rebels & Outlaws

ISBN 9781906958008, 320p, £12.99 / $25

Handbook for Rebels and Outlaws is a book about freedom. Written for intellectual swashbucklers-men and women who are radicals in politics and infidels in religion-warriors who hammer the stake of fear into the heart of tyranny-this volume belongs in select book collections, between the black magic and the pornography texts.

Contents: Blasphemy; Terrorism (History and Practice); Megaterrorism (Biological Weapons, Chemical Weapons, and Nuclear Weapons); Survivalism and Weapons of Mass Destruction; Non-Violent Resistance (Hunger Strike, General Strike, Civil Disobedience); The "Temporary Autonomous Zone"; Communications, Clandestine; The Revolutionary Cell ; The Assassin in History; "Dirty War" and the State; Coup d'Etat (Theory and Practice); Secret Police (Techniques and Tricks); Deception in War (Theory and Practice); Guerillas, Partisans, and Asymmetric Warfare (History and Practice); The Urban Guerilla ; The Bandit and Pirate in History and Legend; Mafias and Organized Crime ; White-Collar Crime (Non-Violent Crime); Violent Crime; Tyranny in History (Four Types Of); The Police in History; The Informant in History; Evidence (Physical and Eye-Witness); State-Sanctioned Killing; Torture (History and Practice); Prison and Punishment ; Escape form "Controlled Custody"; Techniques of the Fugitive.

The Cannibal Within

ISBN 186992827X, £7.99 in paper

A work of erotic horror fiction filled with "sacrilege, blasphemy, and crime"—written in a style that is part H. P. Lovecraft, part Marquis de Sade, and part Octave Mirbeau—*The Cannibal Within* is literally "wet with sin, slippery with blood, and slimy with fornication."

The Earth is a farm,' wrote Charles Fort.

'We are someone else's property.'

We may think we are special--holy, honored, valued--god's chosen primates--but that is a fraud. The dupes of superhuman forces, we are misfits and abominations. We have no higher purpose -- no savior god died for our sins--we exist, only because our masters are infatuated with our meat.

We have a choice: the evil may be patiently borne or savagely resisted.

. . .one of the most unique horror novels to come along in a long time.' ***Dark Funeral***

For inquires about this and other magical titles visit our website at www.mandrake.uk.net
or call Morgan for a catalogue on (01865) 243671
email mandrake@mandrake.uk.net
or write to: PO Box 250, Oxford, OX1 1AP (UK)

The Way of the Odin Brotherhood
Jack Wolf

ISBN, 978-1-906958-53-4, Paperback Original, £9.99/$16.99

'Would you know more?'

It began with a simple question, sent from an unknown e-mail address, and it kindled the fires of a quest that would take him on a journey of discovery spanning several years; a journey that would lead him closer to the enigmatic secret society known as the Odin Brotherhood.

Continuing a quest for understanding which had been started by his mentor years earlier, and following a trail of cryptic clues and mysterious lore, Canadian author Jack Wolf set out on a journey into the workings of this largely undocumented secret society. Accompanied by a mysterious informant known only as Crow, he embarks on a series of adventures that will ultimately draw him closer to penetrating the history, lore and secrets of this elder pagan fraternity – an entity which has existed for nearly six hundred years.

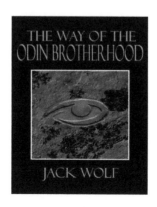

9 781906 958633